DATE DUE

GAYLORD			PRINTED IN U.S.A.

Promises Kept

Promises Kept

Bonnie Ball O'Brien

Illustrations by
Dean Shelton

Bonnie Ball O'Brien is a masterful
narrative writer. This was evident in
her previous book, a biography
of Harry P. Stagg, and it is even
more fully demonstrated here. In
addition to her writing skills, she
has extensive training and experience in the fields of education
and religion. Her husband is
Chester C. O'Brien, executive
director, Baptist Convention of
New Mexico.

BROADMAN PRESS
Nashville, Tennessee

4255-88
ISBN: 0-8054-5588-4

Dewey Decimal Classification: 920
Subject heading: CHRISTIAN BIOGRAPHY //GOD—WILL

Library of Congress Catalog Card Number: 77-80945
Printed in the United States of America

Dedication

To my husband,
Chester Cowan O'Brien, Junior,
whose promises are also
kept.

Introduction

From the creation of Adam until this present moment in time God has entered into covenant relationships with man. In almost every case the pact was conditional: God kept his promise, or agreement, as long as man fulfilled his.

The ancients thus faced the Red Sea, sinful multitudes, dens filled with lions, reluctant kings, false prophets, foreign cultures, and dire illnesses without fear. The knowledge of the certain promise of God to be with them sustained and bolstered their courage through every vicissitude.

The completion of the New Testament canon in no way ended God's dealings with man. Indeed, the coming of the Holy Spirit, the divine paraclete, enabled man to enjoy the constant presence of God in his life. There is nothing on earth quite as beautiful or as completely compelling as life lived on this level. It sparkles the eyes, softens the heart, hardens the purpose, enlarges the vision, and deepens the soul!

The vignettes presented in this book are capsules of such lives. Strong and valiant, they have overcome serious illness, disappointment, timidity, cultural opposition, the oppression of alcohol, parental objection, and penury to keep their promises to God. I present them as beloved friends whose lives have touched my own, and in doing so, broadened my awareness of God's various dealings with man.

Contents

1.
A Promise Kept
Blanche V. Simpson

At the turn of the century, a young family moved from the state of Illinois to a frontier area near Raton, New Mexico. The cattle ranch they settled on boasted few necessities, and no comforts of life. Their house, lighted by kerosene lamps, was heated by coal and wood. There was no indoor plumbing. And while their food supply was adequate, the variety was sorely limited.

Of stern New England ancestry, Frank Oscar Simpson carved out of the rugged land a bare existence for his growing family. Life was hard and sober. It was a serious business; a matter of sustaining one's family with nothing left over.

Katherine Olive Richardson Simpson, daughter of a respected physician, dug in and did her share in making a home for Frank Simpson and the eight children she bore. Intensely devout in her Christian faith, she became a vital part of the young First Baptist Church of Raton. Each Sunday found her driving the team of horses into town five miles away, loaded down with young Simpsons. Evening services for the family were out of the question; the horses could not make two such trips in a single day. Mr. Simpson did not have time for this part of his family's life.

But Kate did! And each evening in the flickering light, she eagerly gathered her large brood about her and read from Bible storybooks by the hour. No sooner had she completed one than they would beg for it to be read again. And then, when she closed the book, her children knelt by her chair and she taught them to pray.

Blanche Simpson came West with this young family when she was only three years old and quickly absorbed all the vital Christian training her mother so lovingly provided. When she was twelve, her father's cousin came for a two weeks' visit. A missionary to British East Africa, she had come armed with pictures taken on the mission field. There was a thrilling story connected with each one—a conversion experience, an answer to prayer, a changed life. Although Blanche had heard about missions through her church, this was her first contact with the missionary challenge. Too, she had never faced the question of Christ's place in her own life.

During these days, Blanche realized for the first time that she needed a Savior. She also understood, young as she was, that accepting the Savior included the lordship of Christ in her life. This troubled her greatly, and one night as her relative told a convincing story of answered prayer in the life of an African boy, Blanche blurted our irreverently:

"Oh, those things just happen!"

The cousin did not rebuke her, but her look, so straight and penetrating, went straight to Blanche's young heart. She got up, left the room, went to her own room and locked the door. Alone, she wept her heart out. And then she knelt by her bed and prayed. She asked for forgiveness, and realized, as she prayed, that God seemed to be saying to her . . . "But I want your *life,* too." When she finally came to the place that she could say, "Yes, Lord, you can be the Lord of my life as well as the Savior of my soul," she found infinite peace. From that night forward, she knew that God wanted her to be a missionary. There was no question about it. And her heart was at rest.

Although this experience occurred Thanksgiving Day in 1912, Blanche was unable to be baptized until the following March. A huge snow dumped forty-nine inches of white mountainous drifts all over the area making the roads into Raton completely impassable. They did not go to church or to school until the month of March when the melting process finally began to clear the icy hills away. They ran out of all food except beans and white flour. Consequently, they simply ate beans and bread three times a day! But the first service she was back, and was baptized.

Although Blanche had no doubts about her call to missions, she nevertheless told no one about her decision. Appeals for foreign missions were rarely heard by her during those days. But the real reason she kept that knowledge locked up tightly in her own heart was that her father was not a Christian and she knew he would actively oppose her decision.

During the next years, however, Blanche gathered every scrap of information she could find about foreign lands. Included were pictures of the people of those faraway places and any other information that would in any way guide her in preparation for missions. All those dear treasures she hid in a box in the barn under a stack of empty feed bags. When she had a chance, and no one was looking, she would slip to the barn and pore over that material and pray that the Lord would help her prepare for his work. One day as she made her way to her sacred place, she discovered to her horror and heartbreak that the box had vanished. She could only assume that her father had found her

cache and destroyed it. She dared not inquire about it. It was an anguishing loss.

When Blanche was about fourteen she received permission from her parents to remain in town on Sunday afternoons and nights with friends in order to attend the Baptist Young People's Union and the evening worship services. Much needed training was acquired as she participated on the programs of that youth organization. And one event, as exciting as a trip to Europe for the young girl, was a trip to Des Moines, forty miles away, for the three day associational meeting! The church hired a Model T Ford for the occasion and that was the first time Blanche had ever ridden in a car, or taken a real trip. Her pastor "made" her address the entire group on Sunday School work, and frightened to her toes, she spoke. Never again was she afraid to speak before her beloved BYPU.

Added to this training was the private study of the old *Sunday School Normal Manual*. Her pastor gave her examinations and explanations, and would not let her pass any book until she had answered every question to his complete satisfaction.

At last, time came for graduation from high school. Blanche knew that she must make public her decision to become a missionary. Her church and her pastor were not surprised. In fact, many said they had expected it for a long time. Mrs. Simpson was most sympathetic with her daughter's yearnings for service, but feared what her husband might say.

Sure enough, Mr. Simpson argued, scolded, and tried to reason with Blanche. So committed was his daughter, however, that she remained convinced of her divine imperative. She would not be diverted or swayed from that calling she had cherished for years.

Then, her father tried to tempt her. He said he would pay her way to attend New Mexico State University; in return, she would never set foot outside the boundaries of the United States of America!

"I cannot promise that, Father," she pleaded, "for training as a missionary is the principal reason I want to go to college."

He remained adamant and unmoved. But he made a final offer. She could do all the home mission work and church work she wanted. But she would not go as a foreign missionary.

Patiently she explained that she felt her call was from God and she must obey him. Her father had a final statement:

"Well, in that case, you are on your own. From today on, you will have to row your own boat. Don't expect another penny of support from me."

The next day Blanche Simpson left home. She found herself in Raton looking for a job, knowing full well that if she went to college in the fall she would have to make as much money during the summer as she possibly could.

She spent almost the whole day going from one business to another, but no one wanted to train a worker for only three months. Discouraged, she went into a tent which had been set up by her church for revival services. No one was present in that late afternoon hour and she sat down to rest and to think and to pray.

"Lord," she prayed, "I do not doubt that you are calling me, and I am willing to go where you want me to go, but I do not know how. I have tried to find a job, but can't. Show me how to go—and I will go."

When she raised her head, she noticed a Bible lying on a pew nearby. Picking it up she began to pray again:

"Lord, if you want to answer me through your Word, let me open the Bible to the answer which will tell me what I need to know *today*."

The Bible fell open to Matthew 28:19–20: "Go . . . and, lo, I am with you alway, even unto the end of the world." The words stood out as never before and burned their message into her young heart. She knew her prayer, somehow, had been answered.

She thanked God for his promise, and kneeling in his presence, promised him that she would never turn back in what she believed and understood to be his will, no matter what discouragements and disappointments she encountered. Writing this promise down as a reminder, she also penned the date— June 7, 1920—and carried it in her purse until it was completely worn out. Thus armed and reassured, she made her way into the street once more to take up the task of searching for work. She had not walked a half block when she met a lady who asked her if she would consider working in the home of a neighbor who had suffered a heart attack and was confined to her bed. The patient needed general housekeeping done, supervision of her three small children, and care for the patient. Blanche was rather proud and it had not occurred to her that she might be asked to do such menial work. But she remembered her encounter with God less than an hour before and was, in short order, cleaning up three small children and cooking the family's evening meal. She worked for three months at forty dollars a month. And when she left for college, she took almost all of it with her. She faithfully paid her tithe and had only nominal expenses otherwise. One month she spent only seven cents!

In September Blanche arrived in Abilene, Texas, eager to enroll in Simmons College (now Hardin-Simmons University). There were no new clothes in her wardrobe; the only items she had bought were a pair of shoe strings and a box of shoe polish. The women of her home church had given her a shower and provided her with numerous small items and a little cash.

The fellowship she found among the young people equally committed as she, was like heaven on earth. She was happier than she had ever dreamed a human being could be. Mission volunteers went to nearby churches and sang and prayed and spoke. There were noonday prayer meetings. And there were sessions of dreaming dreams together.

The money did not last long. Blanche washed dishes every day from the day she arrived until the day she graduated. She worked at other jobs as well. Sometimes she borrowed money to be paid back later. Sometimes a most welcome gift of money arrived. But never a penny from her father.

Since the financial picture was constantly bleak and nagging, she decided to take the four years of college work in three years and one summer. Even with her frugality and hard work, January of her senior year found her hard pressed.

It was time to register for the second semester's work. She had five pennies, carefully tied in the corner of a handkerchief. She had tried to borrow money in several places, each time without success. At last, in desperation, she went to the school's treasurer to see whether she might borrow enough from the student loan fund to complete her undergraduate education. To her dismay, she found the fund depleted and was told that there was, in any event, a waiting list of eleven people ahead of her. No hope was given.

That meant there was no earthly source for help. More tenaciously than ever she clung to the Lord's promise to her. She prayed and claimed it all over again, and head held high with assurance, she went to the library and simply signed up for the full course of study along with all the other students. Then she returned to the treasurer's office and took her place in line with the other students who were waiting to pay their bills. She had her five pennies, and God's promise that if she would go he would be with her even unto the end of the world.

A friend, knowing her financial predicament, saw her in line and said, "Oh, Blanche, did you get some money?"

"No, not yet," the confident student replied as she took another step toward the treasurer. "But God is not going to fail me."

About that time, Mrs. Sandefer, wife of the president of the college, walked into the treasurer's office. Seeing Blanche in line, she approached her and said,

"Blanche, are you going to need any money this spring to finish school?"

"I certainly am," the girl replied, inching closer to the time and place where her tuition must be paid.

"Well, the WMS of the First Baptist Church in Abilene has decided to create a scholarship fund for a worthy girl, and they have authorized me to invite you to use this scholarship until you graduate, if you so desire."

Blanche's heart sang with joy as she gladly and gratefully accepted the offer. And by the time her conversation with Mrs. Sandefer was terminated, she was face to face with the treasurer for the second time that morning. He pushed a check toward her, smiling broadly as he did so. She endorsed it and returned it to him. That check paid her tuition and expenses for the rest of the year including her graduation fees and diploma. There was even money for books. God had again supplied her every need.

After graduation and working to get a little fund for her seminary training, she enrolled in Southwestern Baptist Theological Seminary in Fort Worth. A scholarship furnished by one of the WMU organizations of a district in Texas paid for her tuition, board and room, plus allowance for books and piano study. Her days, thus, were considerably easier in seminary than they had been in college. However, never one to waste time or money, she completed the normal three year course in two years and one summer.

Engerly she applied to the Foreign Mission Board for appointment. Everything she had done since she was twelve years old, every intent and motivation of her heart, every sacrifice made, was for the purpose of going to Brazil as a missionary. At last, she had a reply from the Board:

"We deeply regret that we are unable to appoint any new missionaries at this time, due to the indebtedness of the Foreign Mission Board."

Blanche was totally unprepared for that stinging disappointment. God had promised to go with her if she would prepare and get ready. As far as she knew, she had kept her part of the bargain. And he had kept his promise so many times, how could he fail at this supremely crucial time? Was it possible that he had led her this far, only to abandon her? She could not believe that such was the case. God had led. He would continue to do so.

She began to teach school while waiting God's further direction. During the summers of 1928 and 1929 she worked in New Mexico in WMU and Sunday School work. While gathered with five other dinner guests in a Clovis home one evening, she confronted her problem as did the others, who, like Blanche, were unable to go as missionaries because of the financial distress of the Board. They prayed until 2:30 in the morning. Should they, indeed, go to their committed fields of work on their own? It never occurred to them to apply to other boards; they were all staunch Southern Baptists.

Blanche, along with two others, felt that God was saying "Go." Not "Go if you have financial support from the Foreign Mission Board." And so she, along with her two classmates, Floy Hawkins and Blonnye Foreman, made their final decisions that night. They would go. The rest was up to their sender.

Two months later Miss Hawkins sailed for China; two months after that Blonnye Foreman sailed for Brazil. Each went on his own.

Only Blanche was left behind. Night after night she sat at her piano playing softly to herself: "To the regions beyond I must go, I must go . . . "

At last she was offered board and room in the Baptist Mission School in Victoria, Brazil, in exchange for her work of teaching English. She was thrilled that the door was open just a crack and began to pray for steamship passage to Brazil. So intense was her longing and so deep her commitment to missions that sometimes while she would be teaching her classes, her eyes would fill with tears as she struggled hard to regain her composure.

Finally the answer came. A pastor called her and said, "Do you really want to go to Brazil?"

"You know I do," she replied. "I don't think or talk about anything else."

"The reason I am asking," the pastor went on, "is that I have in my hand a check for $500.00 from a deacon in our church. It is for your passage to Brazil—if you are sure that is the Lord's will!"

One month later, November 30, 1929, a jubilant young woman sailed for Brazil from New York Harbor. Again, there had been money only for bare necessities, but gracious friends and mission societies had given her some greatly appreciated help. Her trip home to Raton was, of necessity, brief. Her father, whose attitude seemingly had not changed, received her warmly and even kissed her good-bye—the only time in her life she remembered such affection from him. She never saw him again; he died during her first year in Brazil. Later friends told her how he had bragged about her courage and determination. Somehow, this warmed her heart, as she felt that he had forgiven her for going against his will.

Her ship sailed into the harbor at Rio de Janeiro on the morning of December 12, 1929. A group of missionaries waited to greet her, among them Blonnye Foreman. After a few days of visiting in that area she and Miss Edith West, a fellow missionary, boarded a train for Victoria. It was a twenty-four-hour trip. The scenery was breathtakingly beautiful. The landscape was alternately dotted with cane fields, coffee plantations, palm trees, gorgeous mountains, little houses made of sticks and mud, and numerous tunnels. At every station people were selling cakes, coffee, cooked bananas, and raw fruit. Parakeets and canaries were also offered for sale.

About sunset on Christmas Eve, their train pulled into the station at Victoria. The missionaries, as well as other Christians, were waiting to greet them. It was a heady experience. The joy of reaching her longed-for destination on Christmas Eve was a gift Blanche Simpson would always remember.

Bright and early on December 26, Mr. Reno called Blanche into his office and showed her a set of books she was expected to keep. They looked like pages of doctors' prescriptions! Not only were the notations in Portuguese, she didn't know bookkeeping! Along with the mission director's bad penmanship were added his own special rules of spelling and abbreviating the strange Portuguese words. Looking aghast at Mr. Reno, Blanche remembered that missionaries had to do many things they were not trained for and she simply tackled those books and learned bookkeeping and Portuguese at the same time! She taught a Brazilian girl English in exchange for Portuguese lessons. The girl was only in high school, so Blanche had to select her own books for study, assign lessons to herself, and outline her own course of study! Miss

18

A Promise Kept

Simpson further had to insist that the girl correct her pronunciation because it was considered rude to correct an American!

Blanche Simpson reached Brazil with sixty dollars in her purse. Friends in the States had bravely promised support. However, the Great Depression suddenly had that nation in its tight, strangling grip. The first year she was in Brazil, she received only five dollars! After she had been in Brazil for six months one of the missionaries left on furlough and Blanche was paid twelve dollars each month for her work. However, she was then charged six dollars for her room and board. This left her, after paying her tithes, less than five dollars a month for personal expenses. Yet, she lived like this for a year and a half. Beginning in January, 1932, she accepted work with the Brazilian Baptist WMU as a field worker, receiving the munificent sum of twenty dollars a month plus traveling expenses. Even so, she was able to save enough so that when time came for her furlough, she had enough money to pay for her own passage home.

When Blanche began to work with the WMU of Brazil she was given a small room in the girls' boarding school in Rio de Janeiro. Rio was much easier to make travel arrangements from, and her field was the whole of Brazil. She felt that all the work she had done up to that point was preparation for this field work and was overjoyed at the opportunity.

And so she began her work with the women—training, teaching, strengthening. She had bought a little organ which she took with her everywhere. It proved to be quite an attraction. She stayed in the homes of the natives who were as generous with their meager store as anyone could possibly be. Often only one or two rooms of the houses would have floors and usually there were no windows. Sometimes she slept on mats stretched out on the floor or on a hard bed. She even learned to sleep in hammocks slung up on pegs in a room or swung between trees outside. She traveled thousands of miles by train, boat, steamer, canoe, oxcart, horseback, farm wagons, and walked miles by foot. On one trip she rode a mule (the same mule) 1,200 miles! On occasion a boat would hit a sandbar and it would require as many as eighteen hours to free it. At other times, a horse would stumble or throw her from its back, causing a delay. Each time, however, she merely considered it an opportunity to witness to whoever was around. No opportunity was missed.

She was accepted gladly and on equal basis with the regularly appointed missionaries. Indeed, there were so few on the fields at that time that each one was considered to be pure gold! She taught books, attended conventions, camps, women's meetings, and the mission meetings. She trained leadership wherever she went and always played the organ, sometimes far into the night. People would walk for miles just to hear her play that amazing instrument. Often a native would carry the organ on his head and walk many miles to have it available. She even held a religious wedding for a couple who had already been legally married by the state, but who wanted a religious service.

Through the cold winds, the beating rains, the blazing deserts, the broad plains, the high mountains, and low swamps, across swollen creeks and through thick jungles she went, keeping her promise to God. Sometimes the people of one church walked with her to the next church, being taught along the way, so eager were they for training and fellowship. They would then return and the people of the new church would do the same. Everywhere she made friends, trained the people, and witnessed always to the power and grace of God.

One night she and her party reached a home late at night. The anticipated hosts had retired, but so overjoyed were they that they sent their children out to get all the neighbors up and to return for a late night service! They couldn't wait for morning!

Once, after having been thrown from a mule, Blanche's back was terribly wrenched. She was seven days' ride from any doctor. It was impossible to have medical care. And so she simply rode on from appointment to appointment on the mule, weeping in agony as she rode, and then pumping the yearned-for organ at night. She never knew the full extent of her back injuries because after a time, the natural healing processes of the body took care of her.

At last, it was time for a much needed furlough. She bought passage on a Japanese ship and landed in Houston, Texas, in December, 1935. There were many changes at home: her father was dead, her mother had moved into Raton and there were new husbands and wives among her sisters and brothers. Life does move on!

During this time of furlough, she was extremely busy in camps, WMU meetings, and conventions. It was while she was helping Miss Eva Inlow, WMU Director of the Baptist Convention of New Mexico, that she received word from Dr. C. E. Maddry that she had been appointed the 400th missionary of Southern Baptists! Her joy knew no bounds. This meant that she would have financial backing now, but most of all—and that which would mean the greatest support of all to her through all the continuing years—she would be upheld in prayer by Southern Baptists around the world. This moral and spiritual aid sustained her in a special way the rest of her days.

In December of 1939 Blanche and her mother found themselves in New Orleans awaiting a ship to return the daughter to Brazil. Things were quite different this time. For one thing, Blanche was not alone as she had been the first trip out, and her baggage was larger! She had some new clothes, a brand-new folding organ, a typewriter and mimeograph machine, a bed with an innerspring mattress, and other necessities. And when she arrived in Brazil, she was asked by the Board to spend six months in intensive language study which she had not been able to do during her first term of service. She had room and board in the home of Dr. and Mrs. L. M. Bratcher and could now live as other missionaries.

In addition to her language study, Blanche prepared a second volume of handwork patterns for use by children's workers. She had published a first volume during her first term which had proved to be very successful and there was an urgent need for more. This gave her a valuable respite from the intensity of language study.

Blanche was to continue her WMU work as before and soon started out on another trip, accompanied by her permanent helper and traveling companion, Zilda Azaredo de Silva, a young Brazilian who had graduated from the Baptist Girls' School in Rio. Zilda directed the Vacation Bible School work and taught the YWA groups on their travels. It was hoped that this training and responsibility would make it possible for Zilda to be the leader of a traveling team while Miss Simpson trained another later on.

After the Brazilian Baptist Convention met in January 1938, Blanche and Zilda left for a trip up the mighty Amazon River to visit the Amazon River fields. Taking an ocean steamer, they spent three weeks sailing through dense tropical vegetation, across wide expanses of water, and by houses built on poles ten to fifteen feet high, with water surging by underneath. There were canoes, boats, and islands of grass floating downriver. Sometimes men pulled the grass to feed their cattle, which were awkwardly corralled on the boat.

They landed in Belem where they worked a week and Zilda was inoculated against typhoid fever. Blanche had already had the shot and the trip farther up the river made anyone going there susceptible. The trip was to require two more weeks. But four days out of Belem, Zilda developed a fever. She was taken off the boat at Manaus with a 104 degree temperature. The doctor was called. Blood tests were run. The report was awesome: typhoid fever!

Mrs. Clem Hardy, the missionary in whose home they were staying, was a nurse. She told Blanche that she would teach her how to take care of

Zilda—and so, for seventy days and nights, Blanche gave Zilda medication every two hours. Mrs. Hardy gave shots, sometimes as many as six daily. In the course of the disease, the suffering girl ran three courses of fever, each lasting twenty-one days, but with intervals of a week of normal temperature and sinking spells. By the time she finally began to improve, her mother and brother arrived, and took her home in a woefully debilitated condition.

At Porto Velho, Blanche had the privilege of teaching black Jamaican natives in the English language! They had been brought to Brazil's interior for the purpose of laying the railroad and many who remained were Baptists.

The party stopped at every village along the way to teach and conduct evangelistic meetings. At one spot, the mosquitoes were so bad the people brought towels to the services and slapped them away. It was reported that the mosquitoes were so bad in that area that a horse, running for his life through the high brush could be killed in a single night by the mosquitoes clinging to him.

Blanche stopped in homes built high over the water, made of palm leaves and resting on stilts. She ate boiled fish and mush made from mandioca meal. The mush was cooked in the water in which the fish had been boiled. She was served this with such regularity that she never again enjoyed fish.

It was on this trip that she met Carmen Franklin, the nine-year-old daughter of an American couple. Blanche asked if she might take Carmen to rear and educate, knowing that her chance for education in the interior was very remote. She enrolled Carmen in the Baptist Girls' School in Rio. (In 1950 she and Carmen came to the States where the girl was enrolled in Wayland College. There she met and subsequently married a Brazilian youth, the ceremony being televised. Moving to Washington, D. C., he was attached to the Brazilian Embassy. Tragically, Carmen was in a fatal car accident in Manaus, Brazil, in 1975, leaving several children and her husband—and Blanche—to mourn their loss.)

Beginning late in 1939, she began to confine her work to a single state— Rio. Because of the intensive work Blanche had done, interest was created to the extent that girls she had trained were ready to be sent out as itinerant workers during the vacation period.

When the missionaries with whom she lived began their furlough she moved to Italva. She had her dear friend, Señor Nilo Salles, who was a builder, erect a house suited to her needs and then rent it to her. Señor Salles and his wife—also a treasured friend—made her life in Italva supremely happy. Blanche lived between the Salles and the church. It seemed a perfect set up!

She continued to train the girls who went out to serve, bringing them to Italva for orientation, notifying churches of their schedules and travel plans, planning their itineraries, and helping them formulate their programs · They were sent primarily to churches which Blanche herself absolutely could not reach within the year. She firmly believed the emphasis on the training of the Brazilian nationals strengthened the work and helped it to grow rapidly.

On her first birthday in Italva there was a huge celebration! Every family in the church brought a cake. Since she was forty years old that day, they brought forty cakes! They served coffee and everyone cut into the cakes amid great festivity. The Brazilians love *festos* and plan elaborately for such events as birthdays.

Blanche was due another furlough by 1942. But her beloved native country was in the throes of a cruel war. It was not safe to travel by boat. The Germans were busy sinking American ships, and so she delayed her trip—not because she was afraid to go home—but for fear she could not get back to Brazil!

At last, in 1943, she made the trip by plane, arriving in Miami, Florida, and riding the bus hundreds of weary miles to Raton in northern New Mexico. At every rest stop soldiers, many of whom slept on the floors of the crowded buses, were fed first. She often missed meals during those long tiring days because there simply was not time to feed a civilian woman missionary!

In less than ten months she was back in Brazil. The urgent needs of the fields, other missionaries who needed furloughs, and Carmen, pulled her back. With the war still raging and plane reservations given preferentially to military related personnel, it required six tedious days for her to reach Rio de Janeiro.

She began to visit the Baptist school in Campos several times each year. She stayed a week or two each time conducting studies with the Baptist students, especially with the ministerial students and volunteers for special service. But these visits were woefully inadequate. They needed a course of Bible instruction and religious training throughout the whole year. Even though Blanche was working as corresponding secretary-treasurer for the Woman's Missionary Union, teaching in all the regional institutes, attending all conventions and annual associational meetings, and visiting many local churches, she felt a gnawing urgency toward these students who needed training so desperately.

The problem seemed compounded as she visited churches who begged time after time for her to stay longer, to try to commit her to a definite time in the future or to plead with her to send someone else. There was no one to send and no money to provide further help. At last, the plan seemed to crystallize in her heart. She resigned her position with the WMU and asked that a new missionary be assigned that responsibility. She went to the director of the *Colegio Batista Fluminese* in Campos and volunteered her services as teacher of Bible and religious education in the school. She arranged for board and room in the girls' dormitory and spent her weekdays there, returning each Saturday to Italva for her church duties.

She developed two intensive courses of training. The first she called the pre-theological course. A student must successfully complete forty books selected from the Sunday School, Training Union, and WMU curriculum. An average of four weeks, with five hours study each week, was spent on each book. Upon successful completion of this course, the student was eligible to enroll for the theological course, a four-year study in Old and New Testament, systematic theology, homiletics, Christian history, evangelism, missions, and archaeology. She explained to her students very carefully that these were *preparatory* to seminary study. But for those who could not attend the seminary, the courses were basics to service.

Knowing that the students needed to have practical experience and that the churches desperately needed the students, Blanche began to study the map of Rio very carefully. She searched for the most needy mission fields. And in Santa Maria Madalena, about one hundred miles from Campos, she found it! She rented a large house and moved there, ready to start a new phase of her work.

Blanche did not move alone! By late 1946 her household consisted of seven persons. D. Maria de Lurdes, her cook and housekeeper since 1942, went along as did Vivaldina Reis, the youngest child of D. Lurdes. Carmen Franklin moved with her adopted mother. By then Carmen was eighteen years of age. John Xaves, an orphan boy had moved into Blanche's household after his father had died on the streets of Italva. The police had taken John's emaciated form to Blanche and asked her to take care of him "until he dies." They promised to pay for his burial. Blanche had looked at the fourteen-year-old waif who was the size of a five-year-old and her heart turned over at the sight of him. She nursed him back to health and he moved to the new home as well. Then there were Gerson Sá and his sister Teresa Sá, two young children Blanche took into her home because they were starving to death.

The "family" settled into its new home during school vacation. Being temporarily relieved of her teaching duties, Blanche set about the business of starting a Sunday School in her home. Gradually, people came to the house and several made professions of faith. Then, she went to visit a little church in Trajano de Moraes with its seven resident members. They were meeting in a little house which was literally falling down. She asked if they would assume the congregation of her group as a mission—but instead of asking financial support, it would be the other way around!

Blanche offered the contribution of her tithe, which would help them pay rent on a safer place of worship, and help them to support a pastor, if they would call one. They were speechless! The church had been pastorless for fifteen years and they gratefully agreed to each of Blanche's suggestions. Pastor Nilo Salles accepted the call of that church and he and his wife moved into Blanche's already large household and lived there for several years until they could find a place of their own.

By fall, Blanche was ready for school to begin, and began commuting to Campos by train, eight hours (but only 100 miles) away. She would bring her preacher boys out by train on Saturday and they would all return on Monday. The boys were given opportunities to speak in the associational meetings and many doors of service were opened to them. When the reach of the train became inadequate to get them to their expanding fields, Blanche simply bought horses and saddles and paid for pasturage for these animals who grazed away, waiting their weekly mission. The churches grew under the leadership of these enthusiastic youths and the work was substantially strengthened.

In 1950, with the continued heavy schedule—she taught from 7:30 in the morning until 10:50 in the evening every day, graded all the papers, prepared lectures and lesson plans for the many courses, plus the long weekends of train travel—Blanche courageously asked the Brazilian mission for a car! It was immediately granted. (Why hadn't someone thought of it before?) She was thus able to make the trip in only two hours instead of the eight by train. The station wagon was of great value to her. She piled it high with young students on Saturday, dropped them off at various mission points along the way, and then gathered them up for another week of school on Monday.

When her furlough of 1950 rolled around, Carmen Franklin flew to the States with Blanche and was enrolled in Wayland College. Blanche's time was filled to the brim with schools of missions, summer camps, conventions, and associational meetings. She also attended the Baptist World Alliance in Cleveland that year and the Southern Baptist Convention in Chicago.

Back in Brazil, she found her household helping as best they could to carry on her work. There were seventy new students enrolled at Campos. And she began once more her intensive training and commuting. In March and April of 1951 the students reported a total of thirty-nine decisions in their services.

The mission began to help her financially to carry on the extensive work. She was thus able to send additional students by train and to pay them a small stipend as well. This often meant the difference in their being able to remain in school. In 1951 she helped fifteen in this manner on a continuing basis.

The missionary who served as corresponding secretary-treasurer for the WMU was on furlough. There was nothing to do but for Blanche to add this to her already full-time load. Somehow, she managed it. Since she could not travel as she had done previously, because of her teaching responsibilities, she trained girls to do a great deal of the work. She continued this training until 1956.

As her students were married—often to each other—Blanche found herself frequently giving the wedding, baking the cake, and sometimes furnishing the wedding gown and suit. Sometimes children of students were born in her home because there was no hospital and no one else to care for them. Often a baby would be named for Blanche. It would then be taken for granted that Blanche would educate the child!

By 1953 inflation had taken a stranglehold on the student body. Her records show that she gave financial aid to thirty-one students that year. On the campus, built to house 260 students, 1,284 youths were crowded so tightly that some of them had to sleep under a floor of the Administration Building. These quarters were unfloored, there was no place to hang their clothing and no chairs of any kind. Blanche, remembering her own barren days of college life, rented a house in Campos and set up a dorm to alleviate this congestion. Who could study in such conditions!

Sometimes in the house a choir would be practicing in one room, an accordion would be going in another, and a boys' quartet practicing on the patio. People came and went at all hours. It was a busy, much-used dwelling. During this time she began a pre-theological course in the school at Madalena. Her time was dear!

After Blanche's last furlough, in 1957, she plunged into her work once more, mindful of the brevity of time and her promise to keep. Often months would pass when she would not see any English-speaking person. She had truly worked "alone" as far as her own people were concerned on the field—except for God's promise that if she would go, *he* would be with her. And he was! Every step of the way.

A Promise Kept

During that final term of service she helped with the Baptist World Alliance meeting in Brazil and continued her teaching and training, attendance at conventions and associational meetings, as well as her work in her church. She had funerals in her home, she drove emergency patients to a hospital miles away and ministered with her heart full of love for her beloved Brazilians. The sands in the hourglass of service were running out.

At last, it was time to retire! She booked passage for June 1963. But the emotional strain of leaving her life's work was almost more than she could bear. Her Christian friends, with tears in their eyes, begged her to stay.

Woodenly, she went about her preparation to leave. She sold her home to the church. Actually, she almost gave it to them. By the time they had paid off the little amount she charged, the Brazilian cruzeiro was assessed at 820 per dollar. She had bought the house for approximately eight and a half cruzeiros per dollar! The small sum she did realize from the sale went almost totally to her students to keep them in school.

Added to the strain of her last year was the imminent threat of a Communist coup. She kept her car filled with gasoline, maintained a two or three weeks' supply of food, and took her money out of the bank and hid it in her house.

Seeing to everything at once, she paid for the operation much needed by her housekeeper of twenty-one years, D. Lurdes. Then she bought her a little house, as D. Lurdes had nothing of her own, had it repaired and painted. She gave D. Lurdes her washing machine, refrigerator, and sewing machine. There was little for Blanche to return home with.

Various associations invited her for special good-byes which added to her deepening sadness. They always gave her gifts. Her family of students arranged a "family reunion" and so deep were her roots in Brazil—and so unlikely was it that she would ever return—that she faced each farewell with infinite grief and sorrow. How could she ever summon enough strength to leave them!

On the pier in Rio on January 4, 1963, stood a dejected group—former students, Brazilian friends, and missionaries. Pastor Nilo Salles and his wife, and Pastor Jabs dos Santos Leao and his wife, were there to say goodbye. Many of them had never seen the inside of a huge ocean liner, and in an attempt to assuage their grief, Blanche secured permission for them to come aboard and examine the huge ship from top to bottom. They were completely fascinated by it and the luxury of life afloat!

When the gong sounded for all visitors to go ashore, the pain returned in all its wracking intensity. The last good-byes were said. As the ship lifted anchor and slowly moved away from shore, the Brazilian friends of a lifetime gathered in a group on the dock and began to sing in Portuguese:

> God be with you till we meet again!
> By his counsels guide, uphold you,
> With his sheep securely fold you;
> God be with you till we meet again!

> Till we meet! Till we meet!
> Till we meet at Jesus' feet;
> Till we meet! Till we meet!
> God be with you till we meet again!

Blanche stood on the deck alone and watched until their faces became one with the horizon, indeed, until the horizon itself seemed to disappear.

"Wasn't it only *yesterday*, Lord, when I first strained my eyes *toward* this same horizon, trying to ferret out some bit of land? . . . Could the years have passed so quickly . . . could I now be old, facing retirement . . . could I really be leaving them, never to return, to work with them again? Oh, God! let it be a nightmare . . . let me soon awake! Oh, God!"

She bought a mobile home so that she and her mother could spend the summers at Glorieta, New Mexico, and soak up all the spiritual blessings there. She continued her service in the States, working in camps, schools of missions, and traveled wherever she could to tell the story of God's work in Brazil.

After three and a half happy years with her mother, Mrs. Simpson entered the presence of her Lord. She had taught Sunday School classes at the First Baptist Church of Raton for forty-five years.

There were no further ties to keep Blanche in Raton after her mother's death. She wanted to find a good missionary church where she could serve, in an area large enough to afford mission opportunities, close at hand, without too much travel. She also needed to be near good physicians. She decided that Amarillo, Texas, fulfilled all her requirements abundantly, and moved her mobile home to that city where she joined the great First Baptist Church.

On hearing Miss Simpson speak for various gatherings in that Panhandle area, one could only wonder, "What else could she give? She has given everything she had." But there was more.

In 1972 Blanche Simpson deeded her last possession—her mobile home— to the First Baptist Church of Amarillo. It was equipped as a medical-dental clinic and taken down to the Mexican border. Committed Christians from that church began to serve the physical and spiritual needs of those people. Later, others made the pilgrimage to conduct evangelistic services, to hold Bible schools, and to visit. Eventually a church and a pastorium was built with their own skilled hands. A pastor was secured to minister on a full-time basis and the friends from Amarillo continue to go at periodic intervals. They taught the people to make certain crafts which could be sold for a little profit, thus lifting their standard of living. All because Blanche Simpson had something else to give.

She went to live in the Mary Trew Home in Dallas on Thanksgiving Day, 1972. She often recalls the question put to her before she first went out to Brazil without any means of financial support: "Aren't you afraid to go *that* way?" And her answer always came back clear and simple: "No, but I would be afraid to stay at home in disobedience to what I felt was the clear call of my Savior."

Throughout Miss Simpson's long years in South America her heart often sang the words of the well-known hymn:

> Darkness may o'er take me and my song forsake me,
>   But alone I never shall be;
> For the Friend beside me promised he would guide me
>   And will keep his promise to me.
>
> He will keep his promise to me,
>   All the way with me he will go.
> He has never broken any promise spoken;
>   He will keep his promise, I know.

And Blanche Simpson kept hers. Abundantly.

2.
Working Under Mandate
Estes Monroe Hardy

There is a dearly held legend among the Baptists of Wales to the effect that while the apostle Paul was living in his own house in Rome, though under guard (Acts 28:30–31), two youths from Wales appeared in that Italian capital city to study. They came under the influence of Paul and were present when the second letter to Timothy was written. Paul, the legend continues, mentions them in his closing message to the young preacher and calls them by name, Linus and Claudia (2 Tim. 4:21). They allegedly returned to Wales when their educations were completed and began the first Baptist church in their native land!

Down through the centuries the saga ran, until at last Medford York became pastor of that church. In the 1800's, however, Pastor York emigrated to the United States where his son and his great-grandson became ministers of the gospel.

A granddaughter became the mother of Estes Monroe Hardy. One evening, after revival services in Grandfather Hardy's church, young Estes—twelve years old by this time—was deeply troubled. The evangelist had been preaching only a short time and up to that moment had had no visible results to his ministry. That night Jimmy May had preached from Romans 5:1, "Therefore being justified by faith, we have peace with God through our Lord Jesus Christ."

Unfortunately, Estes had no such peace. He was absolutely miserable! His own father had been engaged in a revival meeting some miles away and had slipped in to get some much needed rest at home. And while everyone else was asleep, Estes walked alone through the deep Bermuda grass for what seemed an eternity. He must have walked miles, circling the lawn, back and forth through the lush grass, deeply convicted of his great need of Christ. At last, the lad simply said, "Lord, you can have your way." There was no other way. And he felt infinite peace. The Scripture was true! It was a private transaction between himself and God.

But he had to share the good news! Although it was midnight or more, he

rushed inside, woke his sleeping family and shared the experience with them. "We had a revival at midnight!" Mr. Hardy recalls. There was reason for great rejoicing.

George B. Hardy, Estes' father, was a well-educated minister, having been schooled at Burleson College, Baylor University, and Southwestern Seminary. When he was pastor in Washington, Arkansas, he was chosen as representative of their minister's alliance to meet Charles Taze Russell, founder of the Jehovah's Witness movement, in debate. The topic of the debate was the doctrine of hell.

Mr. Russell was to be entertained in the Hardy's home the day the rules of the debate were worked out, and fourteen-year-old Estes was extremely interested. He remembers even today the warning his father gave Mr. Russell: "We can discuss anything except religion. I don't want you to mention your religion in front of my family." And he didn't!

However, before the test was conducted, Mr. Russell paraded the streets of the town with a large placard on which were the words "Good News—No Hell!" It created quite a sensation.

There were to be five encounters between the two men. However, after the second debate, Mr. Russell received an urgent telegram from his home in the East, requesting his immediate return.

Curious, those involved in Washington began to trace the source of the telegram. They discovered that a black youth, working in Mr. Russell's hotel, had been paid ten dollars to send the message to the debater! In reality, Mr. Russell had arranged his own departure! He died six weeks later from a heart attack while returning home by train from another engagement.

During Estes' growing up years, the camp begun by his grandfather York had great influence on his life. People from all over Pike County, as well as the surrounding countryside, flocked to Sweet Home Camp Grounds for spiritual strength and training. The camp functioned about seven months out of the year and was located near the York homestead. Services were held morning and evening, and often during the free hours the men built shacks to house the growing numbers of people.

When Estes Hardy was seventeen years old he felt the urgent call to preach. But he wouldn't consider it—or so he thought. Perhaps he remembered young Jimmy May whose own ministry had been cut short by his untimely death. Estes would always remember that he, Estes, had been the only known convert in that youthful minister's brief period of service.

But God wanted Estes to preach. And when he married Zula Mae Kelley, he often awakened her at night, preaching in his sleep!

During this period of trauma in his life, a revival was being conducted in his wife's home church. The pastor and evangelist visited with him and "accused" him of having been called to preach. They urged him to preach for the church on Sunday night, and he agreed to do so. He made his commitment to preach the very night he presented his first message.

Almost immediately, the church at Caney Fork in Shawmut, Arkansas, called him as pastor. He was ordained in August, 1923, when he was twenty-one years of age. Meanwhile, he taught school at Center Ridge. The next year he became pastor in Alpine, Arkansas, where he also accepted a teaching position.

After three happy years in Alpine, the family moved to Bills Town where Estes and his father organized the Baptist church. The Hardy's only son was born while they were there. (A few years later, singer Glen Campbell was born in the same residence. Estes Hardy's brother taught Glen to strum a guitar, and Glen never forgot this kindness. He pays the Hardy family visits during the hunting season when elk, deer, bear, and turkey wander all over the New Mexico mountains.)

The next pastorates were at Blue Hatcher and Bokchito, Oklahoma. The latter pastorate was in Choctaw country and although most of the church constituents were Anglo, there were three Indian families.

After about four years in Oklahoma, Estes began to grow very weary. He ran an afternoon fever. He lost weight and developed a nagging, hacking cough. No one had to tell him what was wrong. He had already lost his father and a sister to the menace of tuberculosis. A doctor was needed only to tell him how long he would live.

"It's in the last stages," the doctor said. "You won't live long enough to get to New Mexico." And so, at the age of thirty-three he had the solemn verdict: less than six months to live.

But he could *try* to get to New Mexico's salubrious climate! It never occurred to him to give up, and so with the car filled with gasoline and five dollars in their possession, the young Hardys started working their way west.

Mr. Hardy sold Bibles along the way. They picked cotton wherever they could and finally reached Kellerville, Texas. Miraculously, it seemed that the farther west they moved, the better Estes felt!

He found some carpentry work to do in Kellerville which lasted about three months. Finding no Baptist church there, the preacher-carpenter announced a revival meeting. Services were conducted under a huge, spreading oak tree. After the services were over, a church was duly organized with eleven charter members, including eight for baptism. To this day, the church at Kellerville retains the enviable record of giving more on a percentage basis to mission causes than almost any other church in that area.

But it was not all church and carpentry in Kellerville. There were days when Estes did not have the strength to do anything at all. His wife bravely came into the picture, selling hamburgers from their makeshift home to help her ailing husband eke out their meager livelihood. The country was trying bravely to wrest itself from the terrible throes of the depression, and hard times were the general lot of Americans.

When an oil well burst forth in Kellerville, however, it was a harbinger of better times. Estes remembers the day well. It was on Monday, and a lady's wash was completely ruined by the brand-new gusher!

During their three months in Kellerville, Mrs. Hardy made thrifty use of her time by canning fruits and vegetables. When the family picked up again and started west, they had a little reserve of food available for their needs.

They traveled over dusty trails on their narrow tires, and working along as they could, arrived at last in Farmington, New Mexico. They were eager to settle down in some place of spiritual need where they could serve and where Estes could get well.

Someone told them that the Lindrith area was such a place. Getting into their car once more, and backtracking south and east, they reached the small community at last. To their amazement, they found that the nearest Baptist church to the east was in Espanola, seventy-eight miles away; to the south the closest place of worship was at Bernalillo, ninety miles away. Farmington to the west and Pagosa Springs, Colorado, were also ninety miles away! They had indeed found a place of great need, untouched previously by Baptist witness.

They set up housekeeping in a log cabin with a dirt floor and a dirt roof. In his spare moments, the recuperating minister repaired a house they were to live in during the cold winter months. Because Lindrith is encircled by the continental divide, weather conditions can be very abrupt and severe. That winter proved to be just that; snow seemed to be everywhere!

The very first Sunday in their new locale, the four Hardys made their way to the Union Church operated under the Presbyterian Board. They worshiped there until May 9, at which time the greatly recovered Baptist preacher had located nine Baptists, and they started a Baptist church. They found space in the old log schoolhouse, and joyfully met together week after week. At the end of the first year, Estes had baptized seventeen converts into the fellowship of the new church.

Sundays were the bright spots in the week. Every other day found Mr. Hardy grubbing sage brush, picking up potatoes, or laboring at anything else he could find to do for a dollar a day. But with all their thrift and hard work, the day came when there was no kerosene to light their lanterns and no money at all. While pondering what they would do, they heard a knock at the door. When Mr. Hardy opened the door, he hardly knew what to think. A man whom he had seen only one time stood before him.

"I was passing by your house," the man began, "and something told me that you needed money. Here is ten dollars!"

The Hardys were not surprised at God's quick provision for their needs. They discovered later that their benefactor, after feeling impressed to give them the money, had gone somewhere to borrow the cash himself, in order to give it to them. He became a charter member of the Lindrith Baptist Church when it was formally organized.

On another day they were completely without food. The children were hungry and Mrs. Hardy's heart yearned to do something to stave off their growing hunger. Never having asked for anything before, they also knew that the man who owned the little grocery store in Lindrith made it a practice never to extend credit to anyone. But, Mrs. Hardy reasoned with her husband, "I can't bear to see our little children this way. Surely, if you tell the grocer our circumstances, he will help."

And Estes Hardy, equally moved, made his way to the grocer and explained their plight. They were doing their best to get the farm together to have a crop the next year; in the meantime, there was no reserve. He had sold his car to get some needed farm equipment, and there was no cash available from any source. Could he, somehow, let them have a few groceries?

Surprisingly, the man relented and gladly gave them what they needed. And, at Christmastime, Fred Chamblee, the gentleman who had so generously left the ten dollars, pulled his cart up to their door and unloaded a side of meat, fifty pounds of potatoes, pumpkins, and turnips!

"The Lord has always been on our side," Estes Hardy declares. "He has taken care of us."

The next year a wonderful crop was harvested. He marketed his potatoes for three-fourths of a cent per pound. He had to pay twenty-five cents a hundred pounds to have them hauled to Albuquerque, but since he had 1,500 sacks, he netted $750. When their pinto beans were gathered, they found, to their delight, a 6,000 pound crop. Selling at six to eight cents a pound, the Hardys found that they had some money to tide them over.

Eventually the preacher bought eighty acres of land, then 160 more, at one dollar per acre! He leased additional land for grazing and timber, sometimes up to 2,000 acres. Year after year he and his son, Truett, and their "hands" farmed the land in a successful manner. He became respected in his community as a businessman, but his farming enterprise never for a moment got in the way of his major commitment, pastoring the Baptist church at Lindrith.

For many years he accepted no salary whatever. Church funds were given largely for mission causes *in other areas*! When Estes realized that there were communities all over the mountains with no gospel witness at all, he began to leave after his own morning services at Lindrith, walk to a schoolhouse during the afternoon, which might be as many as nine miles distant. He would preach to the people waiting there, walk back to Lindrith, and preach for the evening worship service. When asked why he didn't go by horseback, he simply replied, "Because I could out-walk any horse I ever saw!" And with a chuckle added, "When I got tired of walking, I ran!"

Each Sunday afternoon he went to a different schoolhouse for services, thus serving five congregations by himself. He walked to Red Lake, to Arroya Blanco and to the Largo schoolhouse. Sometimes when he went to Regina, eleven miles away, he would climb on his tractor and take off down the dirt road. There were poor roads at that time to the other places. Although he often walked through mud (he would leave his shoes at the door and preach in his stocking feet), snow, and rain, he never failed to get back for his evening services at Lindrith.

He learned that in Chama, sixty miles away, there was no church. He found a ride to take him to that beautiful mountain village, conducted services, established a Sunday School, and proceeded to return home—by foot! When reminded that it was a little unusual for a preacher to walk sixty miles in the United States to his appointment he said, "I had to do it. The Lord told me to. The Lord's business has always come first with me. I don't try to argue—I try to agree. I figure his way is best." This was to be the motivating force through all his ministry: if God said to do it, Estes Hardy simply tried. He worked under divine mandate.

Mr. Hardy has a good working library, much of it inherited from his preacher-father. It was carefully boxed and brought to New Mexico on their trek west and is deeply treasured. During the long, cold winters he studied diligently after the tedious days of labor. He lay on the floor before the crackling fire, and by its light, studied into the night.

The Jehovah's Witness sect began to threaten the peace of Estes' valley and he recalled the revival years before when seventeen candidates were presented to the Malpine, Arkansas, church for baptism. One young girl came from a Jehovah's Witness background. Her father was so violently opposed to her being baptized into the Baptist church that he threatened to kill her and the preacher as well! When Brother Hardy asked her whether she intended to go through with her decision, she reaffirmed her position, but expressed concern for the preacher's safety. Her pastor would not be deterred, however.

The congregation gathered on the banks of a stream and the minister saw the father of the threatened girl standing about one hundred feet away, behind a rail fence. He had his shotgun sticking through the fence and pointed straight at them! Estes had everyone stand in a place of safety. The other sixteen candidates waited well away from the site of the baptism. He took the girl into the water, baptized her, and nothing emerged from that rail fence. During the time that the rest of the group was baptized, the girl's father simply slipped away. "I asked the Lord to check that part of it," Estes says quietly today.

That occurrence in another state, his father's experience in the two debates with Russell—founder of the Jehovah's Witness sect—and firsthand knowledge of their beliefs and operation convinced Estes Hardy that they espoused "the most dangerous teaching on the market today." When they began to infiltrate the Lindrith area, Estes spent the winter in intensive research of their beliefs, as they related to the truths of the Bible. As a result, he authored a splendidly written booklet, *The Scriptures Disprove Watchtower Claims,* to refute the devastating doctrines of that group. It sets forth methodically the basic tenets of Jehovah's Witnesses and shows by substantial scriptural refutation the errors of each teaching.

Since the doors of the First Baptist Church of Lindrith were first opened, they have never been closed to worship. When about two-thirds of the population moved to the West Coast during World War II to work in the shipyards, however, the situation was a little strained. Somehow, they were able to keep things going.

The building itself required about two years for completion. They dug a basement first, walled it in, and then used those walls as a foundation for the superstructure. The first pulpit stand was handmade by the pastor. An excellent carpenter, he chose white pine for that important piece of furniture. All the work was done by volunteer labor, with each person contributing what he could in time, money, and skill. It was on a "pay as you go" basis. "We've never owed anyone anything but the gospel," their pastor said. "We have never been in debt."

For many years they had no baptistry in the church itself and just baptized all over the community wherever they could find "much water." Eventually one was constructed in the church. Cement was poured on the bottom and the walls were cemented all around. With excitement, they prepared for their first service using the baptistry. They filled it to capacity on Saturday. About five minutes before time to baptize the next day, the walls collapsed and the water went pouring into the basement! The pastor was very disappointed—all that work, the joyful anticipation of having a proper baptistry at last—and, now, this terrible delay. Mrs. Hardy, more pragmatic, had a word of wisdom to offer: "Now, don't you worry! There must have been someone you were going to baptize who shouldn't have been!" When the service was held at a later date, sure enough, one youth was missing. In thirty years, to their knowledge, he has not entered church again, nor was he ever baptized or affiliated in any way with a church-related organization.

Two or three times after organizing into a church, they applied for membership and affiliation with the Central Association. In those days it required a full day to travel to Albuquerque, the center of the association, via the two rut wagon road. Only thirteen miles, a concrete road from Bernalillo to Albuquerque, were paved.

The suggestion came back: since they were so remote to that area, why not apply to the Colorado Convention for membership. It would be much easier to travel to that state for meetings, and much more convenient for Colorado personnel to visit with them.

In all the years of struggle, Estes Hardy had never asked any person or any association or state for aid for his church. What had been accomplished had been done through the dedication and hard work of the people in the local setting. And now that they were ready to join hands with a larger group, they wanted membership in their own state!

In 1938 this affiliation was worked out and agreed to. The church was delighted. "All the associational missionaries have been wonderfully helpful to us," Mr. Hardy explains. And today, still in the last reaches of the association's territory, it is nevertheless much more accessible by the modern highways and transportation which we enjoy.

Several times, Estes Hardy tried to resign from his church. With some health problems dogging him, it seemed imperative. Most of his congregation, however, had known no other pastor. It was incongruous to think of Lindrith Church, without immediately linking Estes Hardy's name!

At last, the church had no recourse but to accept his resignation. And he stood to preach his last sermon as their pastor in the early summer of 1975. Although he no longer pastors them, his influence and presence are greatly valued as he lives his days among them.

"There are people in these mountains for whom I have prayed forty years," the veteran muses sadly. "This is why it is hard to leave the pastorate—there are some who still are not saved."

A visit to the church at Lindrith is a refreshing experience. The building rests on a hill just off the highway and is surrounded with pinon trees which dot the area. The interior, molded and formed by the love of its constituents, is neat and well-kept. The song service, replete with old gospel songs, which conjure up memories of a distant childhood, is entered into heartily. Occasionally Estes Hardy's deep rich voice is heard as he enters into the music. The service is directed by a young man, a convert from the Jehovah's Witness group. All in all, it is heartfelt religion, tenaciously adhered to by the congregation.

Following the worship services, the door to the church is closed, but not locked. "We never lock the door to the church. We believe it should be left open. Often there are people who get stranded during snowstorms and seek shelter here. One day I came to church and found a horse tied to a pinon tree over there. Inside I found a saddle, and down in the basement a woman was sleeping snugly in her sleeping bag. We invited her to the church services and told her to make herself at home!''

A tour over the countryside reveals several well-constructed houses, built with the skilled assistance of carpenter Hardy! When each of his children married and settled in the area, he helped build a home for them, just as he had done for his growing family years before. When his brothers moved to Lindrith, he helped with the carpentry for their homes ''on the side.''

Outside the pleasant home which he fashioned for Mrs. Hardy, six or eight buildings are in evidence, none are in use any longer except for the wash-house. Picking up an old wooden apparatus, Mr. Hardy smiles and says, ''This was my first plow. I made it just after we moved here forty-one years ago and used it that first year.'' On the other side of the house is an old cultivator resting from years of use. It, too, was made by its owner and now slowly rusts from disuse.

Inside, it is evident that the most important matters on Estes Hardy's mind have to do with the eternal.

''My grandson-in-law, a young preacher, came by yesterday asking my advice. I told him to wear the skin off his nose in his Bible!'' Estes' own father-in-law, a deacon, had told him years before to ''wear out every Bible you can; the more Bibles you wear out, the better preacher you'll be.'' He fervently believes that the most effective sermons are delivered from the minister's own need. ''Before you can ever preach a sermon to others, you must need it yourself. Necessity is the mother of invention, not only in wheelbarrows and wagons, but in sermons as well!''

After preaching in Cuba some years ago, Estes was told that he was the first Baptist minister ever to speak in that village. He was told the same thing after delivering a message in Chama. No doubt many churches in that area of the state can trace their beginnings to the ministry of Estes Hardy.

''I still like to preach as well as I ever did,'' the seventy-five-year-old exclaims. ''Thousands of messages have gone through my mind that I never had time to preach.''

He muses: ''The 'whys' are always revealed later on . . . the Lord's work is not filled with 'whys' but 'whats' . . . God always has something for you to do . . . the search is almost always self-revealing. The main thing is to recognize the Lord's hand; it is present at all times. I have never sought fame or fortune, but the feeling of knowing that you're in God's will is the conquering element of the whole thing.''

When his Grandfather York preached his last sermon, titled "Eternal Life," it was printed and widely distributed among the family and perhaps others as well. Estes still remembers the first words—"All that a man hath will he give for his life . . ." and that subject became one of his own favorite topics from which to preach. His first sermon was taken from Isaiah 55:6: "Seek ye the Lord while he may be found, call ye upon him while he is near." And during his long ministry, topics of great consequence were dealt with: "The Cross," "Eternal Life," "The Value of a Soul."

"The most outstanding thing about my life," Mr. Hardy states, "is that we can't mention any area of life where God hasn't provided abundantly. If it hadn't been for him, something would have gone wrong . . . he has always taken care of us."

In 1972 the *Baptist New Mexico Annual* was dedicated to the Hardys and two others who had made significant contribution to New Mexico Baptist work. Under the Hardy's picture was the caption: "Pastor, missionary, evangelist, counselor, church and community builder are titles aptly describing the life and ministry of Rev. E. M. Hardy in his more than 38 years as pastor of the First Baptist Church of Lindrith, New Mexico. Mrs. Hardy has been his faithful companion, loyal home builder and dedicated co-worker during these years of sacrificial and effective service in a difficult field and through many trying times. The Baptists of New Mexico honor themselves in dedicating the 1972 annual to these two saints of the Lord."

Estes Hardy might add that when one is working under divine mandate, all one has to know is the plan. When one has his orders from God, life takes on its ultimate purpose and meaning. There is no real success outside this pattern of life.

3.
Nat'ani
George Wilson

The tiny child worked with the colorful beads, fashioning them into a thing of beauty, teaching his stubby little fingers to obey each step. His mother, leaning over him with her watchful eyes, moved gently from time to time to help or correct or to teach a new design. Occasionally he looked at her for approval and received it instantly. Her eyes glowed with her love for him and the expression in her face beamed approval and acceptance. And when his father joined them, the warmth of caring was broadened. Few words were spoken; they were not necessary. Their bonds transcended mere verbalization.

Life was simple on the Indian reservation in South Dakota when the century was new. There was a quiet dignity in their unity with nature, in their ancient culture, in their fervent worship. Looking on, one might almost assume it was enough.

Some adjustments were necessary when Jake Wilson, a stalwart Sioux Indian, decided to move into town with his family. Agnes Frazier Wilson, part French and part Indian, gathered her four children and their few possessions and followed her blacksmith husband into Santee, Nebraska, in hope of providing a better life for their children. One by one the children were sent away to boarding school; it was the only way for them to acquire an education.

At last, Agnes began to get her youngest child ready for the journey. George, knowing the intense love of his family for him, and returning it in full measure, stoically made his way to school. He was five years old.

But the noise and clatter! It was almost deafening! People talked incessantly. Sometimes they *said* they liked you or even loved you; but their eyes didn't warm with love and their facial expressions did not always corroborate their declaration. He was forced to use a strange language, English. Since he knew nothing but Sioux, he was more bewildered.

George, observing all of this, and experiencing some of it, was increasingly unhappy in the boys' dormitory where youths of all ages were housed. One night he arose from his bed, gathered his possessions in his short arms, and simply moved across the drive to the *girls'* dormitory! They, he reasoned, were much nicer. He would just live there.

When his presence was discovered, however, he was transported back to his place of departure. He simply could not live in the girls' dormitory. And, so, the years passed.

By the time George Wilson reached high school age, he had developed a very strong interest in music. It consumed him. Paying little attention to the religious teaching in his school, which included Episcopal and Congregational, he formed a band from among his peers. They began to play for dances all over the area. He and his cousin were prize dancers in the ballrooms as well, and this added to their repertoire. But when it came time for him to graduate, he sadly realized that his education was at an end. There was no way he could go to college. It was unthinkable!

During these years his voice had developed to a remarkable degree. It was rich and melodious. He was thus asked to sing for his own graduation exercises from high school.

In the audience on that momentous day was a representative from the Episcopal Training Center operated in connection with the University of South Dakota. So impressed was he by the student's voice that a full scholarship to the Training Center was offered him. There was a stipulation: he would, in turn, become an Episcopal priest.

There was no other door opened to the talented youth. His yearning for higher education was so great that he accepted the offered help. There was little thought as to what the stipulation meant. He was not committed to God, he simply wanted an education.

In this light, perhaps, it was not strange that he continued with his dance band. As he advanced in his studies, it came his turn to serve at High Mass. Since he was always very late returning from his band engagements on Saturday nights, he sent a substitute to fill in for him whenever he had a Sunday obligation. However, he could not always depend on finding one of the students ready to take his duties of High Mass. And he had reached the point in his studies where only one more step was required before he would become a priest. Graduation was very near.

The fateful Sunday arrived. Time for the High Mass came, but George Wilson didn't! He had no substitute to stand in his place on that important day and George couldn't make it back in time. The authorities investigated the situation and discovered the reason for his absence. They felt it entirely unfitting for an Episcopal priest-to-be to be the leader, or even a participant,

of such a music group. Their ultimatum was simple and clearly understood: he would give up the band or he would leave school.

Religion was only a form to George Wilson. It was mere ceremony. It held no meaning. He had studied his lessons and passed his subjects easily. But it was only of the head. And his music came from a more urgent wellspring.

George, thus, left the school. He had no money, but made his way to the Indian Boarding School in Lawrence, Kansas. He found a room to live in and enrolled in the University of Kansas. He chose music as his major and began to be featured in various shows in the area and spent whole summers in his music engagements. He also sang in various churches in Kansas City as a paid soloist. And although he had no feeling for his ancient Indian religion, he found nothing during those days that made him even remotely curious about the Christian faith. Singing was a job he did well, and he enjoyed doing it.

While engaged in his studies, a contest was held for musicians. Madame Ernestine Schumann-Heink, the operatic toast of two continents, was among the judges. A Czechoslovakian, she had made her debut in Graz, Austria, when she was only fifteen years old. Subsequently, she enjoyed a sparkling career associated with the Metropolitan and Chicago Civic Opera Companies.

George, by this time, was well trained in the musical arts. So impressed were the judges by his performance that they proclaimed him winner of the coveted contest. Madame Schumann-Heink became personally interested in the young man and introduced him to the rarefied air of the Chicago Civic Opera Company. She taught him as well and when he opened his mouth to sing ''The Holy City'' his interpretation matched hers in every fine nuance. He sang it with brilliance and exactitude, reproducing his teacher's dulcet tones perfectly. And although musically honed and polished, it lacked the edge of a believing heart.

After receiving further training at the Chicago Conservatory of Music and in New York, George Wilson signed a contract with the Civic Opera Company in Chicago. Their only Indian star, he was billed dramatically as he sang across the United States. He was an immediate attraction. Not only could he draw vast crowds, he sang with brilliance when they arrived.

As the years passed, the nation became his stage. On one of his tours he met an accomplished violinist, Maggie Howard, a Navajo. She was also a splendid pianist. Soon she became George's wife.

He made more money than he realized was contained in the whole world. As he drove from one concert to the next in his dashing Packard Twin-6, he felt as if he had the world by a string on a downhill pull. His smart luggage and expensive golf clubs, arranged neatly in the back seat of his convertible, served to verify his growing success. He was on his way up! There seemed to be no other way he could go. The Chicago Civic Opera Company was making so much money from his concerts that it seemed he could go on forever.

One of the most blazing spectacles in the world occurs annually in Gallup, New Mexico, the Indian capital of the world. Indian tribes from the four corners of the nation converge there to perform their colorful dances. It was inevitable that George would eventually be contracted to sing there.

It was evening. The wildly dramatic Indian dances were over. The chanting, the beating of the drums, the stamping of feet were done. And in the silence a quiet figure rode into the arena seated on a white horse. In subdued dignity they seemed as one, the handsome steed and Rolling Cloud. Dressed in authentic Sioux costume, the double tailed war bonnet covered his hair and the profusion of feathers rippled down his back. The spotlight played upon the scene, picking out the resplendent attire, revealing the moccasins, heavy with beads, and the grandeur of the horse. After the initial flurry of reaction at so impressive a sight, a hush swept across the thousands of spectators as Rolling Cloud—George Wilson—began to sing.

His tones were unbelievably melodious, at once sweet and gentle to the ear and then deep and resonant and strong. Each note, polished and sharpened to

44

its greatest impeccable excellence, began to weave its own web of mystical enchantment around the vast gathering. Caught up in the magic spell, the audience leaned into the music, catching and cherishing every subtle shade of interpretation, every treasured vibration. Never had they heard anything like it on earth. And never would they be able to hear enough.

When the incomparable performer returned to his dressing room he was told that two men were eager to see him. He graciously admitted them. He discovered that one man was Dr. C. M. Rock, pastor of the First Southern Baptist Church of Phoenix, Arizona. The other was his son-in-law, Rev. Harry Stagg, pastor of the local Baptist church.

Together the men began to tell the opera star how thrilled they were with his matchless performance, how perfect and dramatic it had all been. And Dr. Rock continued, "I covet your voice for God, and we are going to be praying that you will give it to him!" The men excused themselves and were gone.

George's next contract was with the fabulous Kimo Theater in Albuquerque. Brand-new and sparkling, the theater intended to provide an extravaganza during its formal opening. They knew Mr. Wilson filled their every requirement. He was billed as the "Sioux Indian Baritone" and his likeness was in great evidence outside the theater, as he was featured bigger than life. And so his concerts began.

One day outside the theater door, a little boy stopped him. Such audacity! But, thus detained, George listened to the child's request. The lad, a Boy Scout, knew that the beadwork of the Sioux Indians was incomparably beautiful and he wondered whether the opera star might teach him that intricate art! George was amazed at this intrusion in his life and rebuked the boy rather roughly. Even though he had two children of his own, by that time, he didn't allow them to force themselves on others! But the boy was persistent.

"Won't you go to church with me?" he inquired. "We are having a revival meeting and you could stay at my house until it's time."

Aghast, Mr. Wilson insisted in knowing why the boy had persevered in his request for George's valuable time. The lad's quiet answer deeply moved the big man: "Because I am a Christian."

Miraculously, George relented. He accompanied that boy to church and was deeply moved by the message of Rev. T. D. New as he sat with the congregation of North Baptist Church (now Fruit Avenue Baptist Church).

The evangelist unwound the truth of his message carefully. "Are you the best person, the best father and husband, you can be?" he queried. He insisted that God would answer the prayers of those who needed help, who needed to be better. "If you pray, believing, God will hear and answer your prayer," he continued.

Who had been telling the preacher about him? He was convinced that someone had! Everything the minister said seemed intended just for him. He knew that his life needed improvement. How did that fellow know?

The message pierced his heart. He returned to his room with the relentless throbbing hounding his every step. He went to bed; still the agony stalked him as a prey. In desperation he arose, went outside and walked up and down the railroad tracks, hour after hour, deep into the night. His head and heart seemed to outdo each other in their throbbing and need. He couldn't shake the trouble off; there was no escape, no surcease.

His spirit lifted not a whit during the physical exercise, he returned to his room and sought a physician. He was declared to be in excellent condition, a fine specimen of manhood. And he knew that his sickness was not of the body; it was of the soul. Somehow he knew that illness was much more dreaded.

He fell on his knees by his bed, remembering that Rev. New had said in his message, "If you pray believing, God will hear and answer your prayer." On his knees he prayed and he believed he felt God's marvelous work of salvation in his heart. He had found the source!

Ecstatically happy, he marveled that a human being could experience such peace and contentment. He understood the power of the prayers of the Gallup encounter and the power of the Word of God. He went to the very next service of the revival, made his decision public, and requested baptism at their hands. When George Wilson was lifted from the symbolic waters of baptism, he stepped to the front of the baptistry and dripping wet opened his mouth to sing. The congregation, mesmerized by the power of his music, heard him voice these words which proved to be prophetic of his life:

> Jesus, Savior, pilot me
> Over life's tempestuous sea;
> Unknown waves before me roll,
> Hiding rocks and treach'rous shoal;
> Chart and compass come from thee:
> Jesus, Savior, pilot me.
>
> As a mother stills her child,
> Thou canst hush the ocean wild;

Boist'rous waves obey thy will
When thou say'st to them "Be still";
Wondrous Sov'reign of the sea,
Jesus Savior, pilot me.

When at last I near the shore,
And the fearful breakers roar
'Twixt me and the peaceful rest,
Then, while leaning on thy breast,
May I hear thee say to me,
"Fear not, I will pilot thee."

Exulting in his newfound faith, George Wilson knew he had to invest his life in something of eternal consequence. Being an entertainer, as good as he was, and as successful as he had become, no longer was enough. Finding an infinite dimension to life, he knew instinctively how to invest his days.

He wired Chicago. He told the Chicago Opera Company's directors that he wanted them to cancel his contract. He was going to give the rest of his life to the Indians of New Mexico, doing everything within his power to win them to Christ. The directors thought he had gone mad; religion had completely diverted him. To no avail they tried to persuade him and at last realized that they had lost the star who had so dramatically enriched their coffers. But they would have the last say, they decided. They made it impossible for him ever to go back on a concert stage anywhere. He would be excluded from every opera house. If he left, he could never return!

Their threats and exclusion affected him about as much as hiding meat from a vegetarian. It bothered him not in the least. He had bigger things on his mind, a larger task to do.

People everywhere made much ado over this "sacrifice" . . . it was unthinkable in 1928 with the nation gripped by the strangling depression! How could he make the trek from the prestigious operatic stage to a remote reservation! Surprised, George never considered it to be a sacrifice in any manner of measurement. "I've gained so much more," he inevitably answered.

Moving his family to Albuquerque, he tenderly won his gifted wife to Christ. Soon they began to minister to their people. They were self-supporting at first, hoping their new venture in faith could be supported by an investment made during the years of his fabulous earnings. He had purchased a print shop in Gallup, and when they began to see their savings drain away during the difficult economic era, he sold his business to somehow thread his way through the rest of the depression. When that was depleted, Mrs. George W. Bottoms, the wonderful Christian philanthropist from Arkansas, became his sole support as she designated her gifts through the Home Mission Board of the Southern Baptist Convention.

George Wilson brought to his new work the same brilliance and power that he had enjoyed as an opera star, but with an important difference. There was now a divine imperative which ordered and glorified the rest of his days.

He and his wife began to visit the pueblos and the Navajo reservation, going where Anglos often could not move as easily. They found their way to Isleta, to Santa Fe, to the Indians in jail, the penitentiaries, the hospitals, and as far north as the Zia Pueblo. They bought a little pump organ and would set it up in a pueblo or on a reservation. When Maggie began to play, George began to sing. Soon a congregation had gathered and he would teach them from God's Word. They listened attentively, many awed by their Nat'ani—their "big man." He was larger than life to them; he was a big man for Christ. Everywhere he went among his people he was called "Nat'ani—Big Man." He wore the title well.

When he visited the children ensconced in boarding schools far from their homes, his heart yearned toward them as he remembered his own days away in a strange environment. Sometimes the boys were taken one by one for a hair cutting and their almost sacred knot was severed. Then they were forced into the shower for a terrible scrubbing, sometimes being helped in that place of ablution by as many as three strong men. Threshing about in alarm, never having been used to much water and never having seen a shower before, they were mortified! Their terror was compounded by the outrage against their dignity. They emerged from this treatment even more silent than before.

George knew the children were lonely as they retreated inside themselves. Wrenched from their close home life, where love permeated the atmosphere, they were thrust into a climate of constant talk. It sounded like incessant clattering to them. And with their finely tuned instinct for love, they recognized antagonism immediately. Mr. Wilson's heart always reached out in sympathy toward those who communicated only with words. There were so many deeper ways, he knew.

Sometimes the Wilsons bought all the food their money would allow and took it along with bedding, water, and literature to the reservation at Alamo where there was a band of Navajos. As they searched for a spot on the windswept expanse or reached a canyon's brim they would set up camp. News of their presence seemed to precede them. By the time they had their campsite erected, wood gathered, and food for the masses bubbling over the fires, the Indians from all over the reservation could be seen joyfully approaching. They came by horseback and by wagon. Some walked. And when they arrived, they set up their own camps and then feasted on the beans, stew, and coffee which had been brought by the missionaries. When possible, canned tomatoes and fruits, particularly enjoyed by the people, were also provided. They stayed as long as the food and other provisions lasted, then all packed up and returned to their homes.

The cooking for these occasions was done in huge lard cans placed over the glowing fires. One day, however, the Indians refused to eat. To their horror, the Wilsons remembered that the wood used to cook the food had come from a tree which had been struck by lightning. The people said nothing, but they fervently believed that the gods had struck that tree. If they consumed the food cooked by its fires, the wrath of the gods would be transferred to them!

Each day George Wilson tediously explained the Bible to them through an interpreter. He sought to help them to get from where they were to where Christ is—and knew that it was a very great journey. He wondered if somewhere in the distant past they had been exposed to the Old Testament's teachings. There were many shadows of it in their ancient religion. Their strong sense of family, the intercession of their priests, and their laws of purification seemed too strong to suggest that their beliefs had come from anywhere else. But, handed down by tradition, by word-of-mouth, from generation to generation, over centuries of time, most of the real truth was lost. George told them that God knew we would forget and, so, he wrote it down so we would have it forever. He tried to show them that Christ was the culmination of everything. It was in him that our eternal destiny resides. It was not white man's religion; it was God's way!

The results were dramatic as many of the Indians followed the Jesus way. But there was no place to baptize them! Eager to follow in obedience completely, they nevertheless refused to come to Albuquerque for such an event. And on the arid reservation, water was almost impossible to come by, at least enough for immersion!

Somehow, God has thousands of ways to accomplish his myriad purposes. The Standard Oil Company had, a few years before, been very interested in drilling for oil on the vast reservation lands. They dug holes everywhere, but they didn't fill them up. One hole produced no oil, but did produce a bubbling spring, a wonderful artesian spring. Constant water flowed from that man-made cavity, and permission was granted for the Indians to use this for their baptismal services. It was always there, ready for their use.

The feeding of the Indians by the missionaries has been an almost spiritual thing. Feasting among Indian groups has been and continues to be extremely important. It is one of their treasured traditions which has been skillfully incorporated into their Christian framework until this day. Everywhere in our Indian Baptist churches the membership eagerly looks forward to the day when they gather for the bountiful banquets.

Maggie Wilson was her husband's constant companion and his unceasing strength in his personal ministry of evangelism. She also served most effectively as musician for French's Mortuary in Albuquerque, playing for funeral services held there. When their fourth child was born in 1932, the family seemed to be complete; everything was wonderful.

George, ever in demand for revival meetings, left his young family, and began one in another city. When their baby was two weeks old, and while the father was away, Maggie suddenly died. George was grief-stricken. Gathering his little family about him he wondered how he could function without her! She was everything to him and to his work. Wracked with agony, he knew he could not care for the children without her help if he continued as he had been doing. The only recourse he could reach with his tortured mind was his music. He would give himself completely to evangelistic singing. He could take his children with him and manage for them himself. He would keep his family together!

Vainly he went about his avowed purpose. He began to accept more of the forthcoming invitations to help in revival meetings. He took his children with him, determined to see to their needs. But it was not as he had thought it would be. He simply could not take care of four small children, one a mere infant, as they needed and provide for their material needs at the same time. With a heart compounded by sorrow he took them to the Baptist Children's Home in Portales and left them there, no doubt remembering his own youthful severing from the warmth of his family home.

In 1935 the pastor of the First Baptist Church of Pampa, Texas, returned home from preaching in a revival. His prime topic of conversation concerned the musician for the meeting. He couldn't say enough! And Geneva Groom, secretary for the church, was intrigued by her pastor's enthusiasm. One-sixteenth Comanche herself, the exuberance over such a talented Indian singer was compelling. And when George Wilson later went to Pampa to sing in that church, they became acquainted. After the revival was ended their interest in each other was sustained and their friendship grew. The next year he mentioned marriage to her. "Oh, I have never thought of getting married," the efficient secretary said, startled. "I have," George replied, with a teasing glint in his eye, "and when I decide to do something, I usually do it." The secret to such security was the fact that he never decided to do anything until he had first cleared it with his Lord.

Geneva knew that they had the same ideas about serving God. Both fervently wanted to do mission work. This, added to her own growing feelings toward him, resulted in an affirmative answer. On February 22, 1936, they were married in her sister's home in Borger, Texas. George was thirty-three years old.

One day George experienced a sudden and frightful attack of appendicitis. As he faced surgery he promised God that if he would let him live he would somehow return with his family to New Mexico and do what he felt God really wanted from their lives. He lived through the operation, which was often "nip and tuck" in those days, and while recuperating at home, struggled to his feet one day and took his and Geneva's four-year-old son for a walk around the block. When they returned George announced, "Well, we'll go to New Mexico and get an Indian Center started."

It was music to Geneva's ears. "I don't remember how long, how many years, I had dreamed of nothing else," she remembers. Joyfully, they gathered their children and their few possessions together and started out in their old rheumatic Plymouth. When they reached El Paso, however, it seemed to have gasped its last. Without sufficient money for its extensive repair, they found they had barely enough to reach their destination by bus.

George was well enough known in New Mexico that he began to give concerts which helped to sustain them while they could get established. His wife found secretarial work at the First Baptist Church of Albuquerque and later with Miss Eva Inlow, WMU Director for the Baptist Convention of New Mexico. While she worked, her husband searched for a house which would be adequate for their needs as well as furnishing a base for the Indian Center. Seeing a "House for Sale" sign on a stucco house on Virginia Boulevard, he entered to find a long front room, plus the usual kitchen, bedroom, and bath facilities. It seemed perfect for their needs. He telephoned Mr. Edwin Egli, the realtor, and explained his needs and purpose. Mr. Egli, a fine layman from the First Baptist Church, told him that the house was actually for sale. "If you would like to rent it for $50.00 a month," he offered, "I will remove the sign and take the house off the market."

Thrilled at finding a suitable place, the would-be missionary knew that if one-tenth that amount in rental had been requested they could not have afforded it. But another layman from the same church, Mr. I. E. Robinette, made the difference. He agreed to pay the rent and even came to help get the house ready for their use! God was providing.

Of course, there was no furniture. Amazingly, when people heard of the proposed center, furniture came from various quarters. For a time there were no drapes over the windows, so passersby thought the house was still on the market and would knock on the door, seeking to rent it!

"Every piece of furniture, every piece of automotive equipment, the house itself—everything—was an answer to prayer," Geneva remembers. And when she was invited to speak for a school of missions in the East she found nothing in her limited wardrobe which would be suitable for such a trip. Unexpectedly, just before she was to leave, a large suit box came in the mail from an unexpected source in Kansas City. A lady had sent a whole wardrobe to Geneva and it fit as though it had been made especially for her! Not one garment was unusable. And every piece was appropriate for her speaking trip. It was as lovely as any clothing she ever owned.

Sometimes it seemed they took two steps forward and two steps backwards almost simultaneously! Sunday School classes were held in their bedrooms and since Geneva served as Sunday School superintendent, secretary, *and* nursery worker, she couldn't give full time to any one of her duties. She left her little ones momentarily one Sunday morning and returned shortly. One little boy, kneeling by her bed, held up a beautiful red doll he had just fashioned. In his other hand he waved a duplicate, only it was gold. She almost wept as she realized that the beautiful red blouse given to her by her pastor's wife, which she had never worn, as well as her gold bedspread, were totally ruined! Another day a child, accustomed to tossing paper or wood on the fire when he became cold, did just that! But the Wilson's gas stove was not exactly the proper medium for that kind of fire. Hastily, she smothered the flames before much damage was done.

The Wilsons did not have a refrigerator and kept any refreshments to be shared with the Indians in the neighbor's icebox next door. When their friends moved away, they offered to sell the icebox to the Wilsons for ten dollars. Somehow it was possible for them to scrape that much money together and the icebox was a great help.

The piano which had been used for their worship services was another matter entirely. It also belonged to the neighbors and when the Wilsons knew that there was no way they could purchase that instrument, they watched their beloved piano being moved across the room and loaded onto a truck. They felt as though an arm had been severed. How could they survive without a piano!

A few days later the pastor of the Edith Street Mission (now Parkview Baptist Church) telephoned them. "We have a piano in our church which has been dedicated to God's use," he told them. "However, it is no longer needed here and I just wondered whether you might be able to use it!" Before the very next Sunday their piano had been replaced. God's timing is exact. They had not been without a musical instrument a single service!

The Indian Center, bolstered by the love and hard work of the Wilsons, grew quickly. Already known widely in the state, Mr. Wilson was instantly able to continue his rapport with the Indian groups of the Albuquerque area. The family, wrapped up in that happy enterprise, considered it no real hardship when one child, mixing muffins for a family treat, was aided by another who held the broken door of the old oven while they baked! Soon, however, there was no question that the house was running over with all the activities, the feasts, the worship services, and, incidentally, the normal family living.

Still, promise for relief looked very remote as they prayed earnestly for larger quarters so they could minister to more people and provide for an enlarged program. One day, Rev. S. M. Morgan dropped by to see them. He had just returned from Atlanta, Georgia, where he had attended a meeting of the Home Mission Board. "I think you can plan on your building," he told them. "I believe it will soon be a reality!"

They were overjoyed and soon were moving into a storefront building at 1506 Fourth Street. They converted the garage into a recreation hall. Thrilled at their "new" facilities, they prayed that some kind of seating would be provided for their place of worship.

One day an Indian, walking down a city street, saw some pews stacked against a building. Curious and interested, he inquired about them. He was told by the man who claimed them that he had been a tent evangelist. "I have gone everywhere in my ministry," he continued, "but now I must retire from that strenuous work." Told about the Indian Center and how greatly they needed benches for their worship services, he was asked if the pews were for sale.

"Those pews were dedicated to God's use," the retired evangelist said. "And if you will load them up and carry them off, they're yours, as long as they are used in the worship of God. And," his voice trailed off as he pointed to his pulpit stand, "you may also have my pulpit!" Overjoyed at God's continued provision for their needs, the benches were carefully placed on a truck and moved to the Indian Center. They were carefully cleaned and repaired and rededicated for the purpose of their original intent—to be used for God's glory.

It seemed, however, that the Wilsons continuously worked themselves out of a building! Before it seemed possible their new location was bulging at the seams with the increased response and the added programs. As their work became more complex, they yearned for a structure designed to fit their specific requirements. At last, they asked that a new Indian Center be placed as a request when the very next Annie Armstrong Offering was received, as Southern Baptists across the nation gave to the cause of missions in America.

Soon they received a magazine in which all the requests were listed. Those which were certain to be granted were listed in a column of white. Next to it a gray column listed the "possible requests to be granted." And last of all, the black column where needs of no hope of fulfillment were printed. The Indian Center was in the gray column!

"We prayed that center into the white column," Geneva recalls. The wonderful stewardship of Southern Baptists made it a reality. The property which they had been yearning for was unavailable. But God has a much better way than ours. The Wilsons were led to a more convenient location on Indian School Road. This land, miraculously available, was within walking distance of the Indian school and on Indian School Road which led to the Indian activities on that school campus. It was near the Indian hospital and much of the Indian population of the area passed by that property regularly. It was a perfect location!

They erected the building in two units at 616 Indian School Road. It made a beautiful base for the mission responsibilities. It was easily accessible to the Indian population of the urban area, to the students at the Indian school, to the patients in the hospital, and led easily to the Canoncito work thirty miles away on the Navajo reservation.

The living quarters were separate from the mission building itself and their auditorium boasted a baptistry! The wonderful Baptist women of Virginia, long interested and helpful in the Indian work of New Mexico, completely equipped the new kitchen. It contained an institutional size stove and was equipped with all the other accoutrements necessary for serving large groups.

In 1950 the new edifice was dedicated to the work of its Builder and the ministry previously engaged in was broadened. Remembering Paul's claim to be "made all things to all men, that I might by all means save some" (2 Cor. 9:22), they sought to help their Indian brothers in Christ find jobs, to enter a hospital when they were sick, and to provide a place for them to spend the night when they were away from home. They fed them and clothed them and visited them when they were ill. But the point of decision for those seeking their help was never whether they would stay for a worship service; it was taken for granted that the spiritual needs always came first. If they decided they wanted food or clothing or other aid, it was assumed that they would also be ministered to spiritually. It was the *Christian emphasis,* after all, which made the Indian Center distinctive from other charitable institutions.

The building was always open. There were all kinds of games for the people to enjoy. Anything which would interest them was provided. And sometimes, interspersed with their worship, feasting, and their games, there was great merriment. One evening two teenage youths were bedded down in a room reserved for those who needed space when they were away from home. The Wilsons heard great shrieks of laughter coming from that room and marveled at the unusual hysteria, so rare among the normally quiet race. The next morning they discovered, to their great amusement, the source of the fun. The Navajo boys were simply not accustomed to sleeping on beds! When they had gingerly climbed in the night before, the soft innersprings seemed to follow every move they made, threatening to toss them to the floor at any moment! Also, the bed was remarkably high to them and they feared falling off if the unruly mattress didn't first expel them. After trying in vain to conquer the monster, they simply did what any good Indian brave would do: they rolled up in blankets and spent the night on the floor, where it was safe. Never were Indians expected to sleep on a soft mattress again!

One of the most meaningful, and heart-rending, ministries the Wilsons performed involved the sanatorium. Too often the patients languishing there had simply waited too long on the reservation for adequate medical care. Trusting in their medicine man to cure them, dreaded tuberculosis only grew worse. By the time they reached Albuquerque for proper care, they were usually considered to be terminally ill. Normally housed in rooms for two or more, they were moved to a single room when death grew near.

The Wilsons visited up to 200 patients each week. They returned as often during the week as it required to visit each one. While George visited the men and boys, his wife looked in on the women and girls. When they were out of town for schools of missions, conventions, or for other engagements, cards were mailed to them. Mrs. Wilson always went by before she left to model any new hat she might have. The ladies enjoyed this tremendously and laughed at the "outrageous headgear" stylish for that day. It served to relieve for the moment the tedium of their wait.

One day Geneva made her way to a single room where she knew a Navajo girl was dying. In desperation she tried to get the message of Christ through to her, but the patient understood nothing. Mrs. Wilson then sent an urgent message for a Navajo Christian to come immediately and translate for her. The gravely ill girl listened attentively, but she was in such a weakened condition that her heavy hair had been cut to try to conserve her waning strength. At last she moved her head on the pillow and her black eyes seemed to look far, far away. "I've never heard of him before," she said weakly. Tragically defeated, Mrs. Wilson and the translator left. "And the next time I went," Geneva recalled, "the room was empty."

As some patients became well, they took the Christian influence to which they had been exposed back to the reservation. And as their families visited them in the sanatorium, the Wilson's service of love impressed them greatly. It made a significant impact on the Indian community.

Periodically, Bible institutes were held at the center. People came from everywhere and stayed for several days for the purpose of intensive Bible study. One day during an institute the Wilsons noticed five men present who were strangers to them. The men sat and listened attentively during the first session and during lunch they were completely amazed at what transpired. Never having sat at a table before, they knew nothing of Emily Post's stringent requirements of conduct. Through courtesy, the meat course was passed to them first. However, the man knew nothing concerning the procedure of getting what he wanted from where it was to where he needed it to be! At last, he simply put his hand under a piece of the meat and lifted it onto his own plate. Immediately assessing the situation, the Wilsons passed the rest of the food in the other direction. The Indians watched carefully and followed the rest of the procedure exactly.

After the meal the men from Arizona spoke with Mr. Wilson privately. They explained that they had heard about him and his religion and had come several hundred miles to learn more. Matter-of-factly they continued: "We want you to come back with us and show our people how to put our feet in the Jesus way."

Sadly, the missionary told them that it was impossible for him to go. And as missionaries across the ages have said, "I have no one to send," he added. The men, desolate, turned, and journeyed home. To present knowledge, no one has ever gone there to show them how to put their feet in the Jesus way.

Although there were many such wrenching experiences, there were multitudes of successes. In an article appearing in the *All-Indian Baptist* in 1947, Mr. Wilson reported contacting sixty-four different tribes through the center, including one tribe from Mexico and two Eskimos. He announced a church membership of thirty-four with thirty-five conversions during the previous two years. In the same paper in 1953, he reported a picnic trip when three cars loaded with people drove to Glorieta to see the new assembly grounds. That excursion created an intense desire on the part of the Indians to become an integral part of the sessions that summer. And in *The Baptist New Mexican* that same year an article written by missionary George Hook was featured. He announced that over ninety students from the Indian school had been under the spiritual care of the Indian center during the previous year. More than fifty, he added, had been converted in the last six months and mentioned the increased response among the Indians of the West to the message of Christ.

In the early 1950's America was engaged in the Korean conflict and many of our stalwart youth crossed the Pacific on a sober mission. George Wilson, Jr., a strapping young man of twenty, joined the Marines. He wrote his family that he was due to be shipped out to Korea, but first, he was granted a coveted leave home. Geneva, in Arkansas participating in a school of missions, cut her engagement short and rushed home. Knowing that their time with their son was to be brief, they wanted to savor each moment.

Interrupting their joyful expectations was a knock at their door. A telegram was handed them. There would be no homecoming, at least, not in the manner they had planned. Their son was dead!

Orders to board ship immediately had superseded the gift of a leave. In the line of his work, George, Jr. had climbed high into the ship to care for some need. Crawling on metal he touched a live wire. Death was immediate.

It broke his father's heart. He was never quite the same again.

In 1953 George Wilson spent two weeks in an Albuquerque hospital. Nothing seriously wrong was discovered in the extensive tests which were run. While he was speaking in Roswell for an RA camp in 1955, however, he suffered a serious heart attack. There was no mistaking that diagnosis.

Emerging from the very threshold of eternity he told his wife in a weakened voice, "I was in a beautiful garden with flowers of indescribable loveliness. The sun was brilliant and shining down on a wonderful path. And then, I saw George, Jr. walking toward me and I rushed to greet him. Just before I reached him he said, 'Not yet, Dad. Not yet.' "

Gradually his strength returned to the extent that he was able to do partial work. When his wife remonstrated with him that he was doing too much he replied, "I surrendered to work as long as I lived—not as long as I felt like it!"

Seeing him change before her eyes, Geneva frequently begged, "George, wait for me, wait for me; don't go yet."

Mustering a smile he would reply, "I'll wait for you. I won't go yet."

Finally, however, at her yearnings for him to remain with her he said simply, "I can't wait any longer. I am so tired."

The doctors had told him that he would never speak or sing again. But he did! From the meeting of the executive secretaries across the South, to state conventions, and local meetings he lifted that magnificent voice and sang. Sometimes he had to be helped to the platform where he would lean against a podium for support. Sometimes he sang from a chair. But at every appearance, the audience was so moved by his voice which had been silvered by so much human suffering, that they could never forget the memory of his music, etched on their hearts forever.

Each such attempt further sapped his ebbing strength, stealing his life from him. But on and on he went. When the time came for the Southern Baptist Convention to meet in Houston he arranged, through his wife's assistance, a concert schedule enroute. Instinctively, she knew that he was in the process of telling his friends good-bye.

All the way to Houston and back he sang, an hour's concert each night. From his chair he wrapped his great heart around his friends as he poured out his soul in music. The notes, tuned with sorrow, at once lifted his congregations in victory and plunged them into grief as they wept as one. They listened in rapturous agony as he sang his theme song, "Nor Silver Nor Gold Hath Been My Redemption," and as he voiced "Grace Greater Than Our Sin." He sang "I Won't Have to Cross Jordan Alone."

And so it was that George Wilson—Rolling Cloud—Nat'ani—bade his Christian friends good-bye. They would not see his likeness again.

That summer the Wilsons attended Glorieta Baptist Assembly during Home Missions Week. Introducing himself to a gentleman across the table one noon, the man said, "I used to know a George Wilson who was a missionary to the Indians in New Mexico." Weakly, Mr. Wilson replied, "I am he."

He had been ravaged by his illness.

In late September of 1958 Mrs. Wilson busied herself one Sunday morning as she planned to go to Canoncito for church. Miraculously a building had been erected there during George's illness and he took great interest in the work. As she noted her husband's unusual weakness, however, she began to protest about leaving him. But George was adamant. "If I can't go, it's your place to go in my stead," he reasoned. There was no changing his mind. She left, reluctantly, driving the Chevrolet Carryall out to the Navajo reservation at Canoncito. She gave rides to people along the way, and after the church services, retraced her tracks. Her riders had no other way to get to church. At last only one girl remained and as they drove along she said, "I'm sorry about Mr. Wilson." Geneva, turning toward her said, "Yes, he's been very ill." But the girl pressed on: "No, I'm sorry about his death!" Alarm shot through Mrs. Wilson, but she replied, "Oh, he's not dead; he's just terribly sick." Her rider didn't utter another word.

Geneva rushed home somehow unusually concerned with a nagging foreboding. Reaching home their daughter, Lonah, rushed out and told Geneva that her father was very ill. Mrs. Wilson looked at her, searchingly. "You mean he's dead, don't you?" Lonah's burst of tears confirmed her terrible fear. Later, Mrs. Wilson learned that the announcement of her husband's death had been reported on the radio while she had been involved in the work to which they were both committed. The Indian girl had heard the news release.

Mrs. Wilson rushed to the hospital where her husband lay, his body inert, without life. On his face she saw a little half smile which she would always treasure and which would somehow be of great comfort. It was the same smile he wore when he saw someone he was especially glad to see or when someone was saying something he was especially glad to hear!

George Wilson had preplanned his funeral to the last detail. Dr. Harry Stagg, who along with his father-in-law, had first mentioned the claims of Christ to Mr. Wilson in Gallup, preached the funeral message. Dr. Stagg by that time had been executive secretary of the Baptist Convention of New Mexico for twenty years. Mr. Wilson always looked upon him as his spiritual father.

Few Indians, however, attended the memorial service for their Nat'ani. It is simply not their way. Deliberately they don't go around the dead. Their deep feelings, held inside, were shown in other ways. The head man of one section of the Navajo reservation took Mrs. Wilson's hand in one of his and placed his other hand on her shoulder. And although he never spoke a single word of condolence, she understood the depth of his feeling and it comforted her. Years later, while standing in a cafeteria line, an Indian man approached her and said, "I want to thank you for the good life brought about for my family when you won us to Christ."

Cards and letters of sympathy poured in from around the world, but the voice which had been used so effectively by God to break the silence in the Indian community was stilled.

George Wilson was larger than life. He had a presence which demanded respect, but more than that, he had a bearing which induced love. In the best sense of the word, he had a wonderful charisma. People of all strata and ethnic backgrounds responded to him as a person first and then as an unparalleled artist. Once after performing at the tribal ceremony in Gallup, George was in his dressing room when he heard noises from a terrible fight which had broken out. He frequently sang for that gathering because it gave him another entree to Christian witness. As the noise continued, George, fearing for his family's safety, left his dressing room and made his way through the melee to check on their safety. As he moved through the mass of people who were angry and incensed, a strange quiet followed in his wake as the people moved respectfully aside to let him pass. "I knew where he was," his widow remembers, "because silence and peace followed him through the crowd. They were not afraid of him; they loved him."

One of Mr. Wilson's foremost tenets as a Christian was his strong belief in the family of God. If we are joint heirs with Christ, he reasoned, then we belong to his family and we should behave in that manner. The occasions when he observed this not occurring in actual practice were bewildering to him. He never understood it at all.

He refused to employ his spirit in useless worry. He simply didn't want to work in that atmosphere! When he had a need or a problem, he simply worked it out with God and left it to him. A loving father, his children never wondered about his care and they adored him. The worst punishment he could unleash on them was his silence. This they couldn't bear. When things were made right, the fellowship was joyfully restored. Interestingly, our own fellowship with our heavenly Father depends completely upon our keeping things right between us!

Mr. Wilson gave himself to his people unreservedly. Even when his ministry involved camping out on the desolate reservations he acquiesced. He didn't enjoy camping, he simply endured it. "I've already *been* camping," he would say to Geneva wryly, remembering his early days in a tepee.

In a special way he gave himself. Anglos have never been a conquered people either in war or through the degradation of slavery. There is no way

Nat'ani

one can fully understand and empathize with those who have. Such felt ostracism cannot be translated into mere words. Being an outcast or a second-class citizen in any society sends up flares of protective covering which can never be comprehended by those who have never "walked in those moccasins." But George Wilson was at one with them. In every way he identified with their innermost longings and fears and needs. Because he felt himself to be an emissary of Christ wherever he went, because he was of the Indian culture in the finest sense of the meaning, his gift of life and talent were magnificent. Dr. Lewis Myers, describing him in his *History of New Mexico Baptists,* called him "a true Indian prophet and teacher and preacher."

Into the fabric of Mr. Wilson's life God chose every thread which was woven together in a marvelous way at his conversion. His provision of an education, his tremendous musical ability and training, his study—meaningless at the time—in the seminary, and his success on the stage—all fell into place when he recognized the lordship of Christ. None of it was wasted. All of it was used.

"I didn't promise to serve God as long as I felt like it," he had said. "I promised to serve him as long as I live." And this promise he valiantly kept until the day he sent someone to serve in his place while he joined his maker.

4.
No Other Foundation
William D. Wyatt

His favorite preacher was conducting a brush arbor revival and young William Wyatt sat in rapt attention. He clung to every word the minister uttered. At the close of the message the evangelist extended a plea, "If you wish to accept Christ, will you please come forward and make it known?"

The youth of eight tender years, clad in overalls, and touched by a deep yearning in his heart, slipped from the wooden pew and made his barefooted way to the altar. However, no one talked with him or explained to him what he needed to do to be saved. At the end of the service, he simply left with his need unsated. Since his parents were not present that night, Bill did not mention his actions to them.

One day Bill's father sold some sheep to a man who then went out to their farm to inspect his purchase. Mr. Wyatt took him back home by wagon and young Bill accompanied them. As the man climbed down from the wagon he turned to the lad, laid his hand on his head, and said, "Son, I hope the Lord makes a preacher out of you!" Perhaps the comment planted a seed of thought and influence, for the growing boy thought a great deal about the ministry during the next few years. One evening at dusk he sat on a rail fence alone and looked out toward the setting sun. "How wonderful," he thought, "if I could be a preacher!" He was not yet a Christian, and so shy and timid was he, that this likely delayed his conversion. "I knew before I was saved that if I became a Christian, I would have to preach," he recalls.

Years passed. He continued in faithful attendance at the church where a Baptist minister came twice each month for preaching services. The other Sundays were shared with other denominations, but Sunday School was held each week in the Baptist church. He sang in the choir of the little Alton, Missouri, church. But during those important years no one ever sat down with him and discussed his need of salvation with him.

As he grew up he was the janitor of the Alton church for a four-year period. He made $2.50 a week. This job, plus his Christian home and church attendance, kept him in close contact with the things of God. He was never

without Christian influence. The Missouri Baptist paper, *Word and Way*, came into his home each week and was avidly read. His parents were staunch supporters of the church. Often the young student thought about his condition in relation to God. "If I am ever saved," he told himself, "I will have to preach." But because of his extreme timidity, the very thought of preaching to people and leading them was almost more than he could imagine.

One of his duties as custodian of his church was the ringing of the bell on Sunday, and to herald special occasions. On Armistice Day, November 11, 1918, he was so excited about the news that every ounce of his sixteen-year-old strength went into the ringing of that bell. He turned it over completely in his jubilation, and then had to climb laboriously to the belfry to turn the instrument over again. The war was very close to the Wyatts. They had lost one son in battle and another had served in the Marines. The end of that martial agony was enough to cause all kinds of celebration.

When Bill graduated from Alton High School he thought he was ready for college. But another grade—a twelfth—was added to the public school system, whereupon the youth simply enrolled again, attended nine more months and graduated once more.

Scholarships in those days for higher education were practically nonexistent. Money was equally scarce. Deciding he would be an electrical engineer,

Bill knew that he would have to work at least a year in order to get started. He went to Kansas and followed the wheat harvest all the way to South Dakota. When that was completed, he found work in Montgomery Ward in Kansas City. But after about three weeks on this job, he received an urgent message from his father: "I have taken a contract to clear land for a banker," the father stated, "and I want you to come and help me."

Dutifully, William left his job in the city to join his father. It was hard work—but work was no stranger to him. By late October he was diligently clearing land and splitting wood. Any such timber became theirs according to the contract, and after cutting it for firewood, they were able to sell it in Alton.

The two spent long hours together clearing the land. It was back-breaking labor which left little time for any other activity, but Bill was earning money for higher education.

One day while father and son were working, the father troubled the waters when he said, "That sure was a good sermon Brother Stroup preached last night at the revival, wasn't it?"

Rebellion began to rise in William's throat, almost choking him. He retorted, "Oh, I couldn't see a bit of sense to it. He didn't prove anything— that there is a God or that the Bible is true."

The father didn't reply, but for his son, the rest of the day was ruined as far as his spirit was concerned. He didn't sleep much that night, either. The next day was spent in much the same aura of conviction and despair. Bill worked hard and long and began, toward the close of the day, to drive the horses back toward home.

"I remember the exact crook in the road," William D. Wyatt says fifty-five years later, "and the rays of the beautiful setting sun, when I said at last, 'Lord Jesus Christ, if you're the Savior, I need saving—and I give up right now.' "

Peace was immediate and complete. But he told no one.

The Alton Methodist church held a revival meeting while school was out during the Christmas holidays. The people worked all day and everyone attended the meetings at night. The Baptists and Methodists, sharing half-time preaching, cooperated during special services. In fact, Bill was secretary for the Methodist's Epworth League and concurrently a member of the Baptist Young People's Union—on alternate Sundays!

One night during the revival while he was in the choir, he noticed his Baptist Sunday School teacher leaving her place during the invitation. His initial reaction as she left her seat was to think, "Well, if Mrs. Eblen joins the

Methodist Church, the Baptists will have to disband!'' But that was not on her mind at all and Bill watched curiously to see what she was about. Momentarily, she made her way into the choir and stopped in front of him!
"Are you a Christian?" she queried.
"Yes, I am," her pupil replied.
Greatly taken aback, she demanded when that transformation had taken place. When he told her that he had been a Christian for about three months, she said,
"Are you ashamed of it?"
"No ma'am," he admitted.
"Then I'd do something about it," she finished matter-of-factly, as she turned to go.
And he did! The following Sunday he presented himself for membership in the Baptist church. He, along with a young school friend and two grown men, was baptized on New Year's Day in an open stream. As each candidate emerged from the freezing waters a blanket was thrown about him. Then they were taken by wagon to a nearby farmhouse to dress.
Six months later Bill Wyatt was in Coldwater, Kansas, riding a butterfly cultivator to cultivate maize while he waited for the wheat to ripen. He intended to follow the wheat harvest once more. One evening, alone in the hay loft with his troubling thoughts, it seemed as though the loft itself extended into eternity. God wanted him to preach! There was no alternative. There seemed to be no choice. And there was no peace. At last he simply said, "You're going to have to help me. But I am willing."
Bill rode back to Alton to tell his parents of his decision. His parents were overjoyed. "I've always wanted to preach," his father confided, "but the Lord never called me. I'll preach through you." And they earnestly promised to help him all they could.
He was still in the grips of his timidity, however. When his mother called on him to lead in prayer before dinner it almost scared him to death. How could he ever preach to a congregation when he could hardly pray at home!
Nevertheless, he entered Southwest Baptist College in Bolivar, Missouri. It was a mountain school, junior college level, and under the direction of the Home Mission Board of the Southern Baptist Convention. It was his serious intention to prepare himself for the ministry and to serve in Missouri. Called upon to lead in prayer at the First Baptist Church one night, he blurted out, "Lord, help us to keep sweet," and when asked to preach he refused, saying, "I can't do it!" But there was a schoolhouse about three miles from Bolivar

where a group congregated Sunday by Sunday for services. A committee from the college arranged for preachers on a rotating basis. One day someone said, "Bill, it's your turn!" He gulped hard—but knew that he must at least try to preach!

A friend who preached about three miles from Bolivar, in another direction, said, "Bill, if you go with me to my preaching appointment, I will go with you for your afternoon engagement if you want some support. I am sure someone will invite us for lunch, and that will be no problem."

Bill quickly agreed and on the appointed Sunday, the two young men walked the three miles to the first Sunday service. After its conclusion, everyone simply left! There was not a single invitation to lunch, and after their early morning walk, the two were more than ready for a home cooked meal. Having no other recourse, however, they began their trek to Bill's appointment, three more miles distant. They found persimmons and black walnuts along the way, which partially solved their most gnawing hunger.

When they reached their destination, Bill, barely eighteen years old, had enough material for his message to have preached a whole revival. He spoke from 1 Corinthians 3:11: "For other foundation can no man lay than that is laid, which is Jesus Christ." It was a significant text for a young preacher's first sermon. And he was through ten minutes later!

In an attempt to help his oratorical skills and develop his speaking ability, he wisely joined the debating team of his college and was also a part of the literary society. By the time he graduated from junior college, and made plans to enter Baylor University, he was eager to preach at every opportunity.

With the need for thrift most pressing, Bill Wyatt hitchhiked from Missouri to Waco, Texas, to begin his work at Baylor. Reaching that city three weeks before school was to begin and during cotton picking season, he found work in the fields. It was agonizing labor, even for the work-brittle youth, because of the back-breaking stance one had to assume for long hours during the day while picking the cotton bolls. He worked long enough to be thoroughly weary in body, but not long enough to develop much speed, picking no more than 120 pounds a day. Since his payment depended on the amount of cotton he picked, he didn't become too wealthy during those weeks.

Staying in the university's dormitory and eating in the school's dining facilities were economically out of the question for Bill. He was invited to attend the little Edgefield Baptist Church by their music director, a student at Baylor. A deacon in the church provided a room for the choir director in his home, and the WMU decided the church could use a janitor—in the form of

Bill Wyatt! There was enough room in the deacon's home for two, and the music director told Bill, "If you have no place to live yet, and will be my roommate, it won't cost you anything." These gestures of friendship and work were most timely and appreciated, and the two young men set up quarters with the deacon's family. The church people were most cordial in offering frequent meals to the two, and one family, the Reddings, were especially benevolent. They had a young sixteen-year-old daughter, Faye, who sang in the choir.

Sometimes Bill had a golden opportunity to preach when his pastor had to be away. And when Dr. J. B. Tidwell's son became desperately ill, Bill taught many of his university Bible classes while Dr. Tidwell remained close to the bedside of his dying son.

Gradually, Bill Wyatt was gaining experience!

When he went home in the summer of 1924 for vacation, his home church at Alton decided they wanted to ordain him before some Texas church decided to assume that privilege. On August 25, the pastor, Rev. J. W. Bays, presided at the ordination. And the young preacher himself preached the sermon, but wept almost all through the message, so deeply moved by this further provision by God. The church clerk, Mr. H. M. Williams, had designed an ordination certificate and it was properly signed. This is a treasured document of the veteran preacher to this day.

Bill returned to Baylor for his final months' work in style! His father had decided that he must have transportation if he was going to be able to preach very much, and had arranged for a secondhand car. Bill learned to drive it the several hundred miles back to Waco! Three days were required for the trip, so he and the car understood each other pretty well by the end of the journey.

All that summer he had been corresponding with Faye Redding. And she had answered, letter for letter. One night, he drove out to Cameron Park with Faye at his side. They decided that their futures belonged together and began to plan for their wedding.

Learning always came easy for the young ministerial student. He could memorize quickly and functioned well academically. Thus, he always enrolled for more courses than were required for a quarter's work, and completed his work at Baylor after his fifth quarter there in March, 1925. Even though he was engaged in outside work as well, he graduated with high honors, one of five in his class to do so. Because half of his work had been transferred from Bolivar, he was not eligible to graduate with highest honors, the level of attainment he had actually achieved.

The next step was obvious. He drove the ninety miles from Waco to Fort Worth to begin his work at Southwestern Baptist Theological Seminary. A friend of his had rented a house and agreed to sublet a small apartment to Bill. With seminary students coming and going continuously, acquiring second-hand furniture was no problem—and using the nineteen dollars he had arrived with, Bill began to set up a livable arrangement.

But he needed a job! Someone told him about Mother Williams who employed seminary students for campus work. She was quite a fixture in Texas. She had led in the building of the girls' dormitory at the seminary and was a charter member of First Baptist Church of Dallas. She was a former president of the Texas Woman's Missionary Union. Coming to Texas from Missouri, as a bride, after her marriage to Colonel Williams, she was a formidable figure.

When Bill approached her about his needs, she told him that she could not use him at all. There were no job vacancies whatsoever. "But since you are here," she demanded, "sit down and tell me about yourself."

She listened with interest as he poured out his story, and then she told hers. She felt a kindred spirit with her youthful guest, a fellow Missourian. After about an hour, Bill stood and bade her good-bye.

"Wait a minute," she said. "You're from Missouri. You grew up on a farm. I have never met a Missourian who didn't know how to work. Get your hoe and report tomorrow!" During his seminary days he worked rather continuously for this most exacting woman. She would sit in her chair and point out work which needed to be done. She grew beautiful roses on campus and sent large boxes of the long stemmed beauties to Faye when she knew Bill was going to Waco. She took great interest in their romance and once told the prospective bridegroom, along with volumes of other advice, "A woman will put up with a lot of things if her husband will tell her every day that he loves her." Fifty years later, Mrs. Wyatt confirms the fact that he has kept that advice extremely well.

Hebrew and Greek were two subjects Bill had to master. He wrote out the vocabulary or syntax on paper and pinned it carefully to the cuffs of his shirt sleeves. As he labored on campus, mowing the vast lawns, he memorized and studied. It worked exceedingly well because his grades were always excellent. In fact, he coached others in those subjects, earning the same amount for tutoring Hebrew and Greek (thirty cents an hour) that he made for pruning Mother Williams' roses!

One day Bill Wyatt decided that he was not going to be a janitor in any church any longer. God had called him to preach, and somehow he would do just that. He dressed for church one Sunday morning and turned his Model T toward Cleburne. He turned onto the first good country road he saw, and found a schoolhouse, where there was no life apparent. He saw a house nearby, drove to it, parked, and got out.

The family was at home. He discovered that they were Methodists and that there was no church nearby. He asked whether he might organize a Sunday School in the adjacent schoolhouse and preach to any who might come. They referred him to the president of the school board of the little Bird community. The man was delighted to know that someone wanted to do such a thing for them.

No one was more ecstatic than the youthful preacher, and just weeks out of Baylor, he began to visit all over that area and to preach to the grateful people who came. He continued this ministry until late summer, when a friend asked him to preach for his mission church in Fort Worth, while he was away in Missouri. "And I might not come back," the pastor added.

Bill agreed to this invitation and arranged for someone to supply in the Bird community. Very soon word came that the pastor was indeed remaining in Missouri.

Before the school session began in the fall, Bill made his last trip to Waco for the purpose of seeing Faye. This time, he planned to return to Fort Worth with her as his bride! Trying to see to everything at once, he had his tonsils removed on Monday, drove himself to Waco on Tuesday, and was married the next day, September 8. His throat was still so very sore that he couldn't say "I do." "But he surely tried," Faye recalls.

Faye had been working all summer and had collected numerous household items which they would need. They were tied onto the Model T and the couple climbed happily aboard and drove back to their apartment, spreading the furniture out over the three rooms and making it home. They had two dollars left after they had bought needed groceries.

Married less than two full days, they made their way to the little mission church for prayer meeting. Bill and Faye, seated in the Gambrell Street Church's mission, listened as they called him as pastor on Thursday night. And Bill Wyatt planned to accept. He asked a friend, however, to preach for him that first Sunday because of his recent throat surgery.

Sunday arrived. The newlyweds made their way to church, excited at the manner in which God was providing a place of service. They waited for the friend to appear to preach, but he never came. "And so I preached," Mr.

Wyatt said. "It was a foolish thing for me to do, but I was their pastor and I was not going to let them down the very first Sunday. I preached that night, too. It took my throat three months to heal."

When Bill picked cotton near Waco, in the summer of 1925, a fellow worker offered to sell him a gabardine suit, which he didn't particularly need, for the munificent sum of five dollars. Bill, the owner of only one suit, bought it and had it altered to fit his needs. The summer before his marriage he managed to buy another suit.

Bill donned his five-dollar gabardine suit when the first converts from his mission were ready for baptism and they made their way to the Trinity River for that meaningful observance. However, during the baptizing, a huge oil spill in the water completely surrounded the preacher, penetrating every fiber in his suit! The cleaners were never able to restore it to wearability. "That took care of one of my suits," he declared ruefully. Thereafter, baptismal candidates were taken to Gambrell Street Church for that service!

One of his fellow students and co-workers on campus was Lee Aufill, who later served with the Home Mission Board for many years. "I have an engagement to preach in Cook County for a revival," he said to Bill one day. "But I cannot go. Can you go for me?"

The student-pastor had never preached in a revival before. It was a sobering request. The fact that the church involved had been disbanded for over two years lent nothing to his feelings of security. "The county associational missionary is trying to revive the work there," Mr. Aufill continued. "You might not even get your expenses paid; you may not succeed at all!"

'I thought that would be a good place for an inexperienced man to start," Bill Wyatt mused, years later. "I could certainly do no damage." He agreed to go, even though it meant leaving his school work and his job in Fort Worth.

The plan was well laid out. He was to go to the missionary's home on Saturday, have dinner with him, discuss the situation, and then the missionary would take him to the church, introduce him to the Saturday night crowd, and leave him for the rest of the week. The plan was followed—up to a point. Arriving at the schoolhouse where the services were to be conducted they found total darkness! There was no hint of life anywhere, except for the two preachers. They waited and waited outside the locked building. "There'll probably be some people tomorrow," the missionary ventured at last, as he started the car to go. "The people have been told about it."

Returning to the missionary's home, the young evangelist no doubt was filled with misgivings about the week which lay so unpredictably ahead.

70

The following day, however, about two dozen people appeared! Bill was delighted. He led the singing, sang a solo, preached, and then extended the invitation—the pattern he followed all week. He stayed in a different home each night, and although not a single unaffiliated Baptist was in attendance all week, nine adults made professions of faith. It was a wonderful week, indeed! Asked to baptize the group, he took the nine candidates down to Flat Creek for the baptismal service. As he was about to baptize the first adult, he lifted his eyes to recite the baptismal message when he saw two men—seminary friends—standing on the bank watching attentively. He was so startled at seeing John Wesley Raley and A. D. Foreman, Jr. in that remote place that he completely forgot his thoughts! He had to start over once more and completed the service without further incident.

The two apologized later saying they should have notified him that they were coming. They were engaged in a revival some miles away, and hearing about the meeting he was conducting, came to the baptismal service.

During his second year at the seminary, Bill pastored three small churches—Flat Creek, Dixon, and Agnes. They gave him a monthly total of thirty-five dollars, but were most generous in loading the Model T with wonderful produce in season, as well as eggs, chickens, beef, pork, and watermelons. Herbert Caudill succeeded him at the Fort Worth mission church.

George Elam, who later served New Mexico Baptists for many years, was a member of the Agnes church. The pleasant association that began between the Wyatts and Elams was later extended to the neighboring state.

Later, the Wyatts began to serve two very fine "half-time" churches, and continued with them until after seminary graduation. Two children were born to them during these years, and with Mr. Wyatt's pastoral duties, his studies, and work on campus, plus his family responsibilities, he required a little over three years to graduate. His grades, however, never faltered, staying in top form all the way through.

Bill Wyatt's prime intent and purpose all during his years of preparation was to return to Missouri and serve a church in his beloved home state. This commitment was so great that as time for graduation drew near, he notified several Missourians that he would be ready to begin full-time work very soon. But nothing at all happened! Not even the hint of an invitation! He was mystified! Every attempt to return was totally fruitless. Ninety long days passed. And still no word from Missouri.

In February, before he was to graduate in early May, 1930, an invitation came to preach for the First Baptist Church in Columbus, Texas. He went down by train and was met by the chairman of the deacons. In those days Bill wore a cap, which added to his youthful appearance. When he alighted from the train, the deacon lifted his eyebrows at the cap, but didn't say anything about it. Later, however, when introduced to a cotton weigher, the man offered, "Well, if I'd been looking for a preacher, I wouldn't shoot at you!"

The church roll consisted of about two hundred and fifty members, and when Bill Wyatt left his hotel on Sunday morning, made his way to the church, and stood before them, they were shocked at his youthful appearance. Tall and slender, he was only twenty-six years old, but had a lifetime of experience in church life and almost three years' pastoral experience. Added to this, he was a ready student, and a diligent worker.

After the services of the day, the deacon chairman escorted him to his train. "If it's all right with you," the man began, "we are going to call you as our pastor on Wednesday night. We furnish a home and $150.00 a month in salary."

The young preacher considered all the ramifications of the last months on his trip home. Could God be leading him to Columbus as pastor? He had so wanted to return to Missouri, but the doors there were all tightly closed. He could only serve where there was opportunity. And the church at Columbus was beyond his wildest dreams.

When he reached home, Faye handed him a telegram. It was from Missouri. "Can you come and preach for us?" it read. But Bill's attention and commitment were now elsewhere. "If God had wanted me in Missouri, he would have arranged it before now," he stated solemnly.

Columbus did call him unanimously and he wired them that he would accept. They moved before graduation day, and he received his degree *in absentia*. For six happy years they served the people in an area of strong Catholic influence. When the baptismal services were held in the Colorado River, the banks would be completely lined with people, curious to see a Baptist immersion!

Calvary Church in Beaumont approached him about becoming their pastor. They were heavily in debt because of an extensive building program and offered him considerably less in salary than he was receiving in Columbus. One Beaumont man said, "He'll never come at the salary we're offering him." But his friend retorted, "If he is the Lord's man for us, he will." And he did!

He began his work in Beaumont on January 1, 1936. They borrowed a truck which belonged to Faye's uncle, to move their belongings. Bill had written a postcard to the church telling them the date of their anticipated arrival. The men were doing quite a bit of work sprucing up the parsonage, and everything seemed to be in readiness.

They arrived according to plan. But they were surprised to find men still working in the pastorium! The men were just as shocked to find the Wyatts ready to move in—but were nevertheless gracious and offered hospitality in one of their homes until the house was ready for occupancy. Bill, preparing for bed that night, found the postcard in his coat pocket! He had, indeed, written them, but in the scurry of the move and the trauma of leaving Columbus, had failed to mail it! Two or three days later, they moved into their new home.

During the next six years the church debts were completely liquidated, a new educational building was erected, the membership grew, and many were baptized into the fellowship of the church.

When the Wyatts moved back to Fort Worth, it was to serve the College Avenue Baptist Church. They discovered among the membership a beloved seminary professor, Dr. Jeff D. Ray. He became his pastor's chief supporter. He wore celluloid collars which were a size or two too large. When he liked the way the sermons were going, he would sit on the edge of his pew in agreement and approval. However, when the line of reasoning went the other way, he settled back "into his collar" and sat immobile. Each year Dr. Ray invited his pastor to speak to his seminary classes, and it was a warm, wonderful contact.

For the first time in his ministry, Mr. Wyatt baptized one hundred converts in a single year at College Avenue! It was such a tremendous thrill to him, and the result of a great amount of hard work and consistent visitation. He visited with the teachers of all the Sunday School classes on a perennial basis and the additions to the church were constant Sunday after Sunday. It was a vivid testimony to faithful witness, conducted week after week, and covered the broad base of the total Sunday School.

When Dr. George W. Truett, pastor of First Baptist Church of Dallas, died, after an illustrious ministry over a period of several decades, Dr. W. A. Criswell of Muskogee, Oklahoma, succeeded him. William D. Wyatt was then asked to accept an invitation from the Muskogee church to conduct a revival. He accepted, and during his days there, the church was convinced that he must be their new pastor.

His four years ministry in Muskogee were some of the most fruitful years in the history of that church. In 1970 a group from the church made an analysis concerning the growth record of their congregation. The results were most remarkable, showing that during Mr. Wyatt's ministry there was a total of 600 additions to the church. It was the church's greatest period of expansion up to the time the survey was conducted.

William Wyatt declined the invitation to join the Department of Evangelism of the Baptist General Convention of Texas. But when the challenge came from the Baptist Association of Tulsa, Oklahoma, he considered it. They wanted him to become their superintendent of Missions.

He had not been at his new task long before he began to miss the pastoral ministry. He was like a fish out of water! It just didn't seem to be his place, somehow.

While he was trying to adjust, he decided to begin doctoral studies in Kansas City at Central Seminary. He had a day off from his duties and the train connections were direct. He could study along the way. Thus, he left one evening, spent the following day in seminars and returned to Tulsa that night.

He relished this renewed association with the academic community. He majored in stewardship and missions, and thoroughly enjoyed the encounters with his two major professors, Dr. W. W. Adams and Dr. W. L. Munsey.

During this period he was invited to preach for the First Baptist Church in Albuquerque, New Mexico. The church was without a pastor. In the state's major city, the population at that time boasted about ninety thousand, and was growing rapidly. The downtown church regularly had six to seven hundred people who found their way into the heart of the city each Sunday for worship. It seemed a wonderful opportunity.

Because of the time difference between the states, the Wyatts were at home on Wednesday evening when the committee chairman telephoned. "We have just called you on the first ballot," he announced. "Unanimously."

The preacher expressed his gratitude and added, "Mr. Morrow, I will need some time to pray about it."

Mr. Roy Crouch, holding an extension telephone said, "The people are awaiting your answer. And we know you have already prayed. We would like your answer now."

Indeed he had prayed. He felt constrained to accept. "I'll come," he told the men. "You can tell the people that I gratefully accept."

They moved in April and began twenty long years of remarkable service, not only in the local church, but in the state and throughout many places in the world.

Very generously, the church agreed that their new pastor might continue his doctoral studies on his day off, and he continued the trips to Kansas City. Because he was near an area of great mission need—the Indian pueblos—he chose to write his thesis about that subject and named the treatise "Christ in the Rio Grande Pueblos."

In this excellent work he traced the history of the Indians of the seventeen Rio Grande pueblos. Beginning with prehistoric Folsom man, who tilled the soil in New Mexico thousands of years ago, working his way through the basket-weaver era, and on to the pueblo period, he sketched the majesty of the Indian culture.

When the Spanish arrived on the scene about 1539 the situation for the pueblo peoples was altered greatly. Not only were new foods and crops introduced by the intruders, but the Catholic religion was brought, even forced, into the quiet pueblos. Many Indians suffered greatly as a result, some were even hanged because they would not accept the new dogma. Others simply incorporated it into their religion. This amalgamation exists even today. The ancient Indian religion remains basic in their hearts and is difficult to uproot.

Because the pueblo lands are considered to be sovereign states, they are not subject to New Mexico law. The constitution of the United States, however, is binding. And even though the guarantee of religious freedom has been ratified in most of the pueblos, it has not always been enforced. The struggle for religious freedom in practice still goes on to a greater or lesser degree even today.

Pueblo lands belong to the people by decree of the Spanish crown. This ownership has been upheld by the US government. The land is passed down, generation after generation, from mother to daughter, in the matriarchal society of the pueblos. Purchase of land for churches—or for any other purpose—is almost impossible to achieve.

The first Baptist work in the pueblos was begun by missionary Hiram Read, en route to California to work. Seeing the great need among the Indians for the gospel and being urged to remain by the territorial governor, he agreed to stay. He preached the first recorded non-Catholic sermon in the state.

The outbreak of the Civil War and other impediments stopped the work later in the century. After many years a new foothold was gained in several of the pueblos as work was begun once more. This usually occurred amidst great difficulty and hardship and resistance. Eventually an All-Indian Camp was begun and a paper for Indian Baptists was started. Gradually missionary work increased.

In some cases, grateful Christian Indians, experiencing the grace of God in their own lives, dedicated their homes to be used as places of worship. The Wyatts themselves were a part of this work as they attended, and participated in, the service one evening in the Jemez Pueblo where the church met in the home of José Rey Toledo. Two of the congregation made professions of faith. Later, the Wyatts received a lovely Indian pottery vase as a memento of the visit.

Sometimes groups went outside their villages for worship in adjacent buildings. Sometimes a governor or an individual would sell or give land for a church to be built inside the pueblo. Some have suffered greatly because of their new faith through ostracism, physical torture, and mental stress. It is not always easy to live for Christ in the pueblo.

While Bill did the research and writing for his doctoral dissertation, the major professors became so intrigued with his subject that they visited the Wyatts, who, in turn, gladly took them on their own personal mission tour. When it came time for his oral examinations, Bill Wyatt knew his subject so well that he just appeared before the examining council and had a splendid time!

When Dr. Wyatt began his pastorate in Albuquerque, the same important areas he had always emphasized were carried into the new arena. Evangelism and missions were always uppermost in his mind and effort. The results in these areas of importance were most impressive. Chairs had to be placed in the aisles for worship services as people responded to the work and ministry of the First Baptist Church and her pastor. In retrospect, Dr. Wyatt reminisces, "We just opened the doors and got out of the way." In actuality, however, the harvest was the result of prodigious work which has always marked the life-style of the man from Missouri. Statistics show that in the twenty-year ministry of Dr. Wyatt, a total of 2,332 were baptized into the fellowship of the church, while 6,452 joined by letter. An amazing average of 439 per year, for twenty years, presented themselves for membership! It was—and is—an enviable record.

As the city grew in all directions, the church established missions in strategic points of the city. Their pattern was most practical in laying firm foundations for work. They built a building, then called a pastor, who began a program of visitation in the area. Each pastor was experienced and began strong churches. Kenneth Chafin was the first pastor of Bel Air (now Del Norte) when it was begun in 1951. Earl Keating, pastor of First Baptist in

Hobbs, New Mexico, was called as pastor of Hoffmantown Church when it was started in 1954. The same wise procedures were followed in beginning Girard Baptist Church in 1955, Belvue in 1958, and Sandia in 1960. Although the Belvue Church was not furnished a building, First Baptist was on their note and paid the salary of their pastor until they were self-supporting, just as they did for each of their missions. In all, 1,098 of their members left the mother church to add personnel to the financial support they were lending. It was truly a mission effort in giving themselves to the city of Albuquerque.

In 1952 Billy Graham and his team conducted their first revival in Albuquerque. Dr. Wyatt was chosen general chairman for the crusade. It was an awesome task. Dr. Graham's staff began to work in the city six months before the services were to begin, advertising the revival, training counselors, organizing the choir, conducting prayer meetings, and all the other minute details which accompany such an endeavor. The general chairman was the nerve center through which all these activities and plans were correlated. In addition to his local church responsibilities Dr. Wyatt helped in the building of a structure which would seat about eight thousand people during the crusade. Senator Clinton P. Anderson helped to get steel frames for the building, at a time when steel was extremely difficult to acquire. Mr. Roy Crouch was also a tremendous help in a multitude of ways and Mr. Chester French, a Methodist layman, signed the note to finance the building of the tabernacle.

It was a tremendous success with four to five thousand decisions being registered. In addition, $7,500.00 was raised for aiding Mr. Graham in his first Korean Crusade and also to help in the care of Korean orphans. When the Graham team returned to Albuquerque in 1975, Dr. Wyatt's previous hard work was appropriately recognized and public praise was given to him.

All during his pastorate, William D. Wyatt was in great demand for preaching engagements. He accepted assignments in Jamaica, New Zealand, Japan, South America, Hong Kong, and the Holy Land. He spoke in evangelistic conferences in most states west of the Mississippi—Utah, Idaho, Arizona, Missouri, New Mexico, Texas, Hawaii, Alaska, California, Washington, and Oregon. He preached in revivals in most of those states, with the exception of his native state, Missouri! Although asked for such help, he was never able to adjust his schedule in order to accept. He appeared before the Southern Baptist Convention's Pastor's Conference on two occasions, and served on various Convention boards, including the Home and Foreign Mission Boards. He served on the boards of Southwestern and Southeastern

Baptist Theological Seminaries. For the last thirty years he has been a member of at least one board. He was chairman of the Texas committee which recommended Dr. W. F. Howard as BSU Director for the state, and nominated Dr. Robert Naylor as president of Southwestern Seminary. He delivered dramatic sermons at Glorieta, Ridgecrest, and Palacios Assemblies many times. He served on the State Mission Board of New Mexico's Baptist convention numerous terms and was its president twice. He also served as president of the Baptist Convention of New Mexico on two occasions. He has written the Bible study for the adult teacher's magazine for The Sunday School Board. He has been a wonderful steward of the gifts which were his by native ability and those he developed by sheer grit and dependence on God.

When asked the secret of a successful ministry, Dr. Wyatt advised: "Try to stay close to God, the Bible, and the people. We have always visited the homes of the people. Rarely did anyone join the church whom I hadn't first visited. I never asked the staff to take my place by a bedside of the sick or the dying; never asked them to substitute for me in soul-winning. And while I encouraged them to do these things, I felt it was my duty."

After his retirement from the pastorate in 1970, he became interim Director of Evangelism for the Baptist Convention of New Mexico for fifteen months. He served as interim pastor at Hermosa Drive Church in Albuquerque for six months and when invited to preach at Chama, in the northern part of the state, he and Mrs. Wyatt began that long trip each week. "We made that journey each week for twenty-three months," he recalls. "We left on Friday and returned on Monday. Sometimes during the week we would do needed shopping for the people of Chama who couldn't get supplies they needed elsewhere. We visited their sick for them in the hospitals of Espanola and Santa Fe. We never got tired of the trip."

After accepting the pastorate of Sierra Vista Church in Belen and serving for about two years, he accepted the pulpit duties of Trinity Baptist, near his Albuquerque home. "There are many lovable people at Trinity," he affirms. And though his seventy-third birthday has passed, he is as vibrant as ever, as erudite, and as inspiring in his messages. He is pouring fifty years of study and experience into these years, truly golden years, of worthwhile "retirement."

Those who have known William D. Wyatt through the years attest to his wisdom, his emphasis on the matters of greatest import and his ability to manage successfully prodigious amounts of work. But an interesting quality has emerged during his years of retirement: In no way has the power of this

78

man been diminished by retirement! He has not leaned on man-made formulas for success and when he stepped out of a full-time ministry, he emerged whole and complete! It is wonderful proof that his foundation was indeed laid on the Eternal Rock!

5.
In a Plain Path
Eva R. Inlow

The young couple, settling down to their first pastorate after the minister's graduation from the Southern Baptist Theological Seminary in Louisville, Kentucky, was eager to do everything and to be everything they should be for the cause of Christ. Coming from the then rather nonproductive farm country of northeastern Missouri, the husband had been college and seminary trained, and so he began to instruct his bride of the requirements of a minister's wife. As a girl, she had been accustomed to running into the nearby fields of her home and claiming whatever horse she found handy, when she required transportation. But a preacher's wife, her husband decided, must be more discreet and so he proceeded to go about the serious business of purchasing for her a gentle steed.

Proud of her docile mount, Mrs. Inlow employed her mount's energies immediately as she hitched him to her buggy for her first visitation efforts. Climbing sedately aboard, she took the reins in hand to guide the horse toward her intended destination. But he had other plans, entirely! To no avail was her struggle to direct him. He headed straight as an arrow for the local bar and stopped dead still, waiting for his passenger to alight. And there she sat, the new minister's wife, buggy and all, in about the worst spot in town! But the poor animal could not be blamed because he had formerly belonged to the town's most celebrated inebriate and simply knew nowhere else to go!

This first deterrent to her work obviously lent little discouragement to the couple, because in a few short years they moved to Nashville, Tennessee, where Dr. R. M. Inlow began to pastor the First Baptist Church. And when an evangelist was invited there to conduct a revival meeting, the Inlow's young daughter Eva was deeply moved by all she heard and gave her heart to Christ.

Dr. Inlow's interest in missions was exceedingly strong, and he engaged missionaries to speak before his congregation at every opportunity. Being in the center of Baptist activity and strength, these encounters were numerous. And Eva heard all of them. Besides, there were always guests in the Inlow home.

One day, however, a missionary from China stood before them. She immediately captured the attention of the pastor's daughter. There was something different about her! She was beautifully dressed! Her clothes fit! They looked as though they were new! They were perfectly coordinated. And Eva, gazing on her in amazement thought, "Can a missionary really look like that?" Perhaps the twelve-year-old had never really looked at a missionary before, but the lady standing before her was so beautifully groomed and striking in her appearance that it changed Eva's whole concept of missions.

Before Eva's thirteenth birthday she felt God's compelling call for missions. He wanted her! And she simply said "I will." Her father was away from home when she made that important commitment and Eva sat down and in her childish scrawl wrote him of her decision. She felt the constraining hand of God for missions, she wrote him, and she must answer. (Years later, Eva found the worn letter among his papers as she went about the traumatic task of sorting out his possessions after his death.)

After graduating from a girls' college in Murfreesboro, Tennessee, Eva made her way to the Woman's Missionary Union Training School in Louisville, Kentucky. Every intent of her heart was toward China and missions. When she graduated with a degree in missions, she applied to the Foreign Mission Board for appointment to China. Those investigating her request carefully went over her portfolio which included her health records. She had the necessary training and she had a call and commitment to go. But their ultimate decision was heartrending: the Board did not feel her health was adequate to maintain needed vigorous work in China. She could not go!

Desolate and disappointed to the core of her being, she felt her call no less. Thus, she applied to the Home Mission Board and in due time was appointed to do mission work in Cuba.

Four happy years passed. She spent two years in Havana and two more sixty miles up the coast in Matanzas. Everyone was wonderfully kind to her, including the superintendent of the Baptist work on the island, Dr. M. M. McCall. But after about forty-eight months in Cuba, her health broke completely. The Foreign Mission Board had been right. She could not live under such constant, difficult work in a strange culture. Sadly, she returned to the States.

Trying to recuperate and regain her strength, while making adequate use of her time, she picked up another degree, a master's degree in the field of education from George Peabody College in Nashville. She was elected youth director for the WMU Department for the state of Oklahoma. And although she was constantly busy there in the much-needed ministry, her job had to be terminated when the depression began to be felt so tragically all across the nation.

She returned to Murfreesboro to teach at her alma mater, Tennessee College. But when she went home to spend the Christmas holidays with her family a letter found its way to her door. It was from Mrs. R. I. Creed, president of the WMU of the Baptist Convention of New Mexico. She explained that their former director, Miss Harriet Gatlin, had resigned and that Miss Inlow had been highly recommended to them by Miss Pearl Bourne, at that time an associate with the Woman's Missionary Union of the Southern Baptist Convention. Mrs. Creed asked whether Miss Inlow might be interested in such a position and whether the committee might be permitted to visit with her during the holiday period.

The group went to Oklahoma City at Miss Inlow's acquiescence. Dr. Inlow, at that time, was pastor there. The committee very carefully explained the work to Eva Inlow. She was delighted with the possibilities of what might be accomplished in that state. Was this where God really wanted her? Was New Mexico the spot where she would use her training and her experiences in Cuba? She knew that God wasted nothing in his great economy and believed that he was leading. It was up to her to be sensitive as he led her in a plain and certain path.

Soon another letter arrived from New Mexico. She had been elected! She remembered a question she had asked as they met together in Oklahoma, "If I come, may I have the privilege of working some with the Indians and the Spanish?" Her work in Cuba had endeared those groups to her and it seemed amazing to her that God might be leading her to an area where she could continue that work to some degree. They told her that she could do all she desired to do among those ethnic groups as long as her own tasks with the Woman's Missionary Union were maintained. The Home Mission Board, they explained, had such work in the state, and would welcome any assistance she desired to give.

Eager to be involved once more in work for which she was so adequately trained, and believing God to be certainly leading, she notified the committee that she would accept their offer. However, her calendar called for a trip to Europe to attend the World Youth Congress and she felt that she needed this trip before she began her full-time duties in New Mexico. Her plan was heartily agreed to and she found her experiences in Europe to be a very wonderful period of "shaking down," of renewal spiritually, and of great inspiration. It afforded her the wonderful opportunity of being with youth from around the world and broadened her awareness of mission need. It gave her stimulus for her new task, motivation which she could not have had otherwise, and in general, made her settling down process in New Mexico much easier.

When Miss Inlow moved into her office in New Mexico she found it barely adequate. The offices for the staff of the Baptist convention were housed above the old Woolworth Building on Central Avenue. There was a bookstore of sorts and four offices which shared one telephone. The staff was small, but extremely dedicated to maintaining their work. The whole nation was in the grip of the great depression, and their salaries were often paid in installments, as funds became available to them. Coming to New Mexico at a salary of $100.00 a month, Miss Inlow sometimes received one-fourth of it one week and perhaps a third the next. It was unpredictable, although paid eventually.

She was given a railroad pass, a token from the Santa Fe Railroad Company. Not having a car, it was indispensable to her travels around the state. Although she was grateful to have a means of transportation in order that her work could be carried out, she was never too excited about the railroad pass! She liked to pay her own way. She had been brought up in that fashion. She discovered that there was no glory at all attached to a dole—but she swallowed her feelings, knowing that there was no alternative at that time.

Often she boarded the train at night after having worked all day in her office. She sat up in a chair car as the train moved through the darkness to some speaking engagement. She conducted all kinds of classes and workshops for women and spoke in associational and state meetings. The people who received her were most gracious and she stayed in their homes and enjoyed their splendid hospitality. Later, when she was able to purchase a small car, and the work grew considerably, the staff began to stay in hotels and she missed tremendously the contact with the people. Philosophically she knew, however, that for everything we gain, we may lose in another area. But perhaps that is a part of progress.

Early in her work in New Mexico, Miss Inlow went to Birmingham for the annual meeting of the state secretaries of Woman's Missionary Union. She met Miss Blanche White, who at that time was her counterpart in the state of Virginia. Miss White asked many questions concerning the work in New Mexico among the Spanish and Indian people. The questions were not asked through idle curiosity, but because of intense concern and love. They were intelligent, purposeful questions which Miss Inlow answered to the best of her ability. She told of the missionaries' work and their joys. She related needs and problems. She shared the struggles, the successes, the setbacks. Miss White listened attentively, seeming in her intensity to be cataloging mentally each shred of information.

When Miss White returned to Virginia she shared with her WMU Executive Board something of the need which Miss Inlow had informed her of. She spelled out the difficulties and the achievements. More than that, she challenged them to do something about it. Thus, those valiant ladies of Virginia, three-fourths of a continent removed from the West, began to give to the mission work among the ethnic groups of New Mexico. There were no strings attached to their giving, they wanted the money to go where the need was greatest. Even though their giving began during the depression years, over the remainder of Miss Inlow's twenty-six years in New Mexico, thousands upon thousands of dollars were directed to mission work in the Land of Enchantment. The generosity is still extended until the present (1977) and wherever one goes in the state of New Mexico there is no surprise when one is told, "This missionary home was made possible by the Baptist women of Virginia," or "This auditorium in which over three hundred Indians meet was a gift from the women of Virginia," or "This Spanish radio ministry is made possible by the generosity of the women of Virginia!" Many fields of service are open today which were begun initially because the mission-minded women of Virginia had a vision of what could be done and simply went about the practical business of funding their dreams.

A source of joy to the staff was their involvement with meetings of the various associations. Miss Inlow recalls, with a hint of nostalgia, the rising early in the morning darkness to prepare for a journey which might involve several hundred miles before she returned home. She would watch through her window for the approaching car lights as her party rounded the corner nearby and moments later would stop at her door. She would hasten out, take her place with the group of state workers, and begin the trip to one of the meetings on their schedule. En route she profited greatly from hearing the discussions of her peers as they talked of the work in the state, their dreams and hopes, and how God was directing.

The associational meetings grew and flourished in those days. The attendance improved remarkably as churches sent more and more representatives to the gatherings for instruction and inspiration. Gradually, more missionaries were employed to work in the state. Dr. Harry P. Stagg had been elected to serve as executive secretary-treasurer of the Baptist Convention of New Mexico in 1938, bringing his remarkable leadership abilities to that office. Things were looking up!

A special time to Eva Inlow was the daily prayer service among the staff members. It was a sharing time, expressing a need here or a victory there. It was a time for prayer, for intercession. It molded the staff together in bonds of love and concern. And until the present day, the members of the staff know that wherever they are, those who are in Albuquerque meet together at ten o'clock each morning to pray for the work in the state and around the world.

One day while Miss Inlow was visiting one of the churches a deacon approached her and said, "You know, the WMU isn't a part of the church at all!" Stunned and greatly taken aback, she replied, "It isn't? How do you happen to say that? We think we are."

He was unbending. "Well, you're not! You don't meet on Sunday when the rest of us do, you take your own offerings, and send them in. You don't even order your literature through the church—you order it all by yourselves. You're just not a part of the church!"

Miss Inlow protested mildly, but began to consider what he had said. She knew that the spirit and purpose of Woman's Missionary Union was church-centered, the constituency from which they drew were members of local Baptist churches, and that their main intent and purpose was to educate in missions and support missions around the world through gifts and prayers and dedication. Not a part of the church! Well, perhaps the appearance might lead one to that deduction. They didn't compete with the Sunday School and Training Union for time on Sunday. They did order their literature separately and take their offerings periodically. Although a part of the church in fact— and a vital part—the appearance must be there, too!

She began to discuss this situation with her co-workers and they decided to request the women of the state to order all their materials through the church along with the other literature. The WMU could bear the expense, if need be, even though the other organizations received theirs as a matter of course. The ladies could then get their supplies from the church instead of having them mailed directly. It was a generous attempt to unify all the avenues of church training.

Several organizations cooperated in this fashion, but Miss Inlow had vociferous reactions from some of her out-of-state friends who felt the change was outrageous and marveled because she had attempted such a thing. Nevertheless she continued her encouragement on the home front and gradually more and more churches found it a convenient way to proceed. Other states, hearing about the drastic innovation, decided to adopt the same process, until it eventually became widely accepted. Today, it is nothing unusual for a church to order such supplies, but to pay for them as well through funds set up in their budgets. The mission offerings have also become churchwide and many of the mission study books and other emphases are conducted on a church basis instead of being presented only to the women and their organizations. Too, many of the auxiliary meetings are held on Wednesday evening before prayer meeting. The offerings and change of lives, the more mission-mindedness of churches, and greater mission involvement are all testimonies to the fact that such participation should be engaged in by the whole church. And in 1976 the Birmingham headquarters transferred much of its business to the Baptist Book Stores who accept orders and process mail-outs to the churches, using the same billing they had employed all along for each individual church. And so the deacon's comment may have been almost an "aside," but it set in motion tremendous changes which proved once more that the leaders in our Baptist life at every level have listening ears and compassionate hearts.

Two or three years after going to New Mexico, Miss Inlow began to feel the need for a summer camp where the youth from all over the state could come for weeks of training. The women, as well, needed a place of retreat and instruction in their work. Looking around for various possibilities, she discovered an opportunity to rent the Presbyterian Camp high in the beautiful Sandia Mountains, just east of Albuquerque. Centrally located in the state, it seemed an ideal, if temporary, solution to the problem. The Presbyterians did not use the grounds every week during the summer, and for a period of two years the Baptists of the state rented their facilities when they were available. In announcing the very first camp, each participant was asked to bring along $2.50 in cash, two cans each of corn, tomatoes, peas, and milk, a box of spaghetti, one pound of bacon, two pounds of sugar, a dozen eggs, and one dozen oranges! They met joyfully together for the first time in 1938, and basked in the fellowship, training, and inspiration they received.

The money they were asked to bring helped to round out the menu for additional food and to pay the rental on the campgrounds. The children literally filled the area to overflowing and it was apparent that the facilities would not provide for the numbers they could eventually anticipate.

Volunteer cooks were employed and the use of the wood-burning cook stoves added to the excitement of camp life. Jimmy Ward, a young man from Gallup, volunteered his services and was available for every kind of job imaginable for a setup of that kind. One evening, when Jimmy knew that hot cakes were on the menu for breakfast the following morning, he asked Miss Inlow if she didn't agree that homemade syrup was much better than the bought variety. She heartily agreed, whereupon Jimmy volunteered to see that the camp enjoyed his own specialty! The next morning when Miss Inlow arrived on the scene she found Jimmy hard at work over the stove, thoughtfully stirring his brew. He called to her rather hesitantly as he explained that the sugar simply would not dissolve. She examined the watery mixture carefully and rendered her diagnosis. The sugar was salt! No wonder it wouldn't make syrup! Poor Jimmy had inadvertently mixed the two sacks containing sugar and salt which were stored side by side. Of course, so much salt could not possibly be thrown away and it was eventually used in seasoning or for other purposes in its liquid state.

During the second year of camp, Miss Bernice Elliott appeared on the scene to help. Miss Inlow had met her in Tatum where she was teaching school. When she expressed interest in the camping program, Miss Inlow invited her to come and assist if she possibly could. She came and made such a difference in the smooth running of the camp. She and Jimmy made quite a team. They never encountered any problem that was too difficult for them to tackle.

It was evident that the Presbyterian facilities were no longer adequate, and even though there were no funds available, Miss Inlow felt that the program was imperative for the training of youth. Too, the momentum they had achieved could hardly be squelched. She approached some Albuquerque realtors and was told that a ranch was for sale in the Manzano Mountains, just south of the Sandias. There was a large hand-hewn ranch house on the property as well as a sizable barn of timber and another building of corrugated tin. It seemed too good to be true—and also completely out of financial reach. Added to this knowledge was the fact that the Woman's Missionary Union of New Mexico is unincorporated and, thus cannot hold property on its own.

Nevertheless, a trek was planned to look over the Sun Valley Ranch. Dr. Stagg accompanied the group and they were shown the enchanting setting. It was 8,400 feet above sea level and almost completely surrounded by stately piñons, pines, spruce, firs, cedars, and aspens whose delicious aroma scented the air in an almost intoxicating fragrance. The group was delighted with the possibilities for a camp in that mountainous retreat and the price of $4,500 which was reached after considerable negotiation didn't seem unreasonable. By careful management of the camps the three previous summers they had a total of $600.00 which could be used as a down payment. Considering this tiny financial base, however, some felt the purchase to be completely unrealistic.

However, after careful discussion with Dr. Stagg, the matter was presented to the State Mission Board for further consideration. The property could be bought in the name of the state convention and the title would be held by it. At least one hurdle was overcome! When the Board met again to vote on the project, the unanimous conclusion to proceed was reached.

Miss Inlow and her co-worker, Miss Elliott, were ecstatic and began the exciting plans for work the following summer. By that time Miss Elliott had become youth director and was an integral part in planning the work for the camp. She was invaluable to Miss Inlow because she fulfilled every requirement one could hope for in an associate.

Little on the grounds at Sun Valley could be used for camping. They were afraid to use the barn and had it torn down. Rafters and rusty nails were much in evidence in that old building and of too great a risk to curious boys and girls. But what would they do the first year?

After considerable consultation it was decided that some of the men and boys would build a kitchen for the camp. Food was an essential. Two or three old wood-burning stoves were acquired and the men built an icebox. They used sawdust to insulate it and an ice company in Mountainair promised to make the sixty-mile round trip to keep it filled with ice. That icebox served a different purpose, however, before camp officially opened. A youth involved in the construction work employed its boxed-in sides for a bed at night as he moved blankets and pillows around it for a good night's sleep.

The most awesome problem had to do with the road which led up to the campsite. It was terrible! Filled with chuckholes and rocks of all sizes and jagged shapes, it was a threat to complete destruction to any car which dared to pass its way. The two WMU leaders decided that the holes had to be filled. And day after day they worked, wearing out their shoes and breaking their backs. They had nothing to work with but their hands, but they tried their best to move the rocks around in such a way that the worst holes would be filled. Every time a car ventured past, the rocks, which had been so tediously planted, splattered in all directions! Added to this were the incessant rains, eroding away at their master highway! Soon it was back in its original state of disrepair.

Other ladies made curtains for the faculty lodge, which would serve as headquarters for the camp. They rented tents in which bunks were erected and they were soon ready for business. They were prepared for two hundred children. When six hundred poured into the camp, Miss Inlow and Bernie began to hammer together more bunks as quickly as they could. The wood they were using was wet lumber and occasionally the sap would spurt into their eyes as they hammered. Long into the night they worked so the children would have a place to sleep. The children were wonderful and cooperative and no doubt it was a camping experience they would never forget. In their spare time the next day, the adults made more bunks!

That first night a wonderful thing happened which made all their work worthwhile. A little Indian girl from the Santa Clara pueblo gave her heart to Christ! And when she returned home she told all her friends what had happened to her. Later, as a token of appreciation and esteem her mother, Maria Naranjo—a famous potter—gave Miss Inlow a beautiful piece of pottery made especially for her. She still treasures it and displays it in her home. As a result of the child's Christian witness, a number of her friends were saved and this helped greatly in the opening up of the Santa Clara pueblo to Baptist work. "As long as I live," Miss Inlow states, "I will remember that little Indian girl as she listened to someone win her soul to Christ. And that, by the way, is what the camp was for—to win them to Christ and to inspire them to mission activity."

After the initial camping season was concluded, attention had to be given to additional facilities. Subsequently, a dormitory was erected, a dining hall

(Manna Hall), a medical building (The Pill Box), and a tabernacle. Through the years other buildings emerged in that scenic mountain setting. Most of the first units were built with volunteer help and Miss Inlow herself was found applying hammer to nail on countless occasions. Gradually, paid help for the kitchen and grounds was engaged and the camp took on all the earmarks of an efficiently run enterprise.

The need for a small building to house male faculty members was urgent in the early days. Miss Inlow and Miss Elliott, the intrepid, unflappable leaders, decided to erect such a building with the aid of some teenage boys. They selected a site among the trees so that when the wind blew from any direction their building wouldn't blow over completely! They found that when they had one wall straight another would be out of plumb, entirely, and when the floor was level in one direction, it would be slanting in another! Nevertheless, it was completed by registration time, and since by some miracle it was still standing, the men moved in. Dr. Fred MacCaulley, with the Home Mission Board for many years, was one of the faculty members. He greatly enjoyed experiences he encountered as a resident of the elegant building he wryly dubbed "The Crack Hotel." His nomenclature proved quite accurate as the breezes blustered through the walls most easily and one could see the light of day from any location inside. Each morning Dr. MacCaulley arose early, walked out in front of his swanky quarters, built a little fire, and boiled his own coffee. He seemed to bask in the days at camp. He returned many times and made valuable contributions to the boys and girls each time.

Miss Inlow discovered that there was a huge army surplus sale in El Paso. She felt it was worthwhile to check it out and she and "Bernie" went down to investigate. They bought a huge walk-in refrigerator for the new kitchen which was being built (and which amazingly was being equipped with huge gas ranges and real aluminum cooking vessels, replacing the faithful lard cans which had been used on the old wooden stoves). And they bought approximately two hundred bunk beds, fully equipped. All of this merchandise was loaded onto trucks and delivered to the campsite. These new additions were greatly cheered by the children, but when shower baths were installed, it was an entirely different matter. The boys had come to camp, and they didn't intend to have all the modern conveniences!

Getting adequate water was a constant problem in the early days. It either had to be brought in from nearby sources or pumped uphill into a large tank. One Monday when Miss Inlow arrived from Albuquerque to set things in motion for the camp, which was to begin on Thursday, Jimmy Ward ran to her car and before she could get out told her that there was no water. A faucet had been inadvertently left on and the tank's water had been drained away almost completely. She started to return to Albuquerque immediately to send word out all over the state that the camp had to be cancelled because of the emergency. Jimmy begged her not to take that measure, to reconsider.

"We can't have camp without water," she insisted. "There is no way we can function for a week with no water!" she emphasized.

But he persuaded her to remain. She and Bernie and Jimmy prayed about their dilemma and the campers came on schedule. Each morning she made an apprehensive trip to the tank and peered in. And on no morning did she find an appreciable difference in the level of water! She has always remembered that experience with gratitude and awe. It was a miracle, a divine provision for their needs.

One day a lady came to the camp to help for the day. She brought her little boy with her. While she was busy he strayed from her. Spurred to wander through the tall, beckoning trees, he was soon lost. He could not be found! Alarm shot through the camp. It was an unbelievable occurrence! It simply couldn't be happening. But it was.

The counselors were all pressed into duty for the urgent purpose of finding that tiny, lost child. As it was a day or so before the camp itself was to begin, there were fortunately no other children to keep track of. They looked and looked, their desperation rising with every passing moment. Miss Inlow telephoned the Forest Rangers for help. They told her that she had the best tracker in the state on the campgrounds, in the person of Mr. Mangum. She explained that Mr. Mangum had been looking for the child, but had lost every trace of him in the thickening woods. They continued to look and while they looked and called, they prayed earnestly.

Meanwhile, one of the former campers from Albuquerque, who had "outgrown" the program at Inlow Camp intended to stay at home and enjoy his brand-new car. Even the invitation to join them as a counselor had not swayed him. But strangely that day he decided just to look in on everyone and see what was going on. He drove past the camp turnoff, however, intending to drive up on his return home. On his way to the Fourth of July Springs, however, his car abruptly stopped. His brand-new car wouldn't budge an inch! He got out, raised the hood, and bent over his motor, trying to ferret out the problem. He didn't have the least idea what to do, and he was some distance from any help. Suddenly, the bushes by the side of the road parted and the tiny, lost boy stepped through them onto the roadway, weeping his little heart out. He had walked for miles through the dense forest, but had finally found the main road. The youth quickly put the child into his car—realizing instinctively what had transpired—and jumped into the driver's seat. He decided to try one more time, just to step on that starter once more to test it out. It sprang to life, instantly! The two turned around in the middle of the road and made as rapid an ascent toward the camp as the old gnarled road would allow. As soon as it could be heard, the car's horn was blown urgently and all those anxious counselors, as well as the child's mother, knew the boy had been located. They emerged to a tremendous reception committee. The lost had been found! "That was another of God's miracles," Miss Inlow declares.

The women of New Mexico were wonderful stewards in paying for the camp as well as in the conduct of its programs. In the beginning, each member of a local WMU was asked to contribute ten cents each month toward the liquidation of the camp debt. Never did the women have to go to the board or to any other source for financial help and eventually the debt was eradicated. Eventually, electricity and telephones were added and the road, which is still no miracle to engineering skill, makes the camp much more accessible in all kinds of weather. The camp continues to be updated as needs arise and as funds are available. In 1976 a beautiful, completely modern home was built for the use of the camp manager who now lives there among the stately trees and cares for the valuable properties on a year-round basis.

One summer as camp was in progress, an escaped convict was thought to be in the area. He was believed to be armed and known to be very dangerous. He would pose a real threat to the children if he suddenly appeared in their midst. Consequently, Baptist laymen, armed with guns, came from surrounding areas and took turns during the night patrolling the grounds. Miss Inlow never did know the names of all the men who came in the night and took over the potentially dangerous, but most important task. It was but one of many tributes to the worth and value in which the camp was held by its constituents. The children, as well as the faculty and counselors, slept soundly, knowing that they were safe from danger.

In the thirty-six consecutive years of its existence, the camp has meant much in the lives of countless young people. Wherever one goes in the state, or the nation, or around the world, there are those serving God in strategic places because of the vision they caught at Inlow Youth Camp. As the campers returned to their churches, the level of Christian strength and influence was felt there as well.

Miss Inlow's service in New Mexico spanned more than two and a half decades of remarkable growth and expansion. Coming in the throes of the depression to a decimated staff and makeshift office provisions, she saw great changes. New church buildings were constructed all over the state. The convention staff was greatly enlarged, and an adequate Baptist Building was erected on Central Avenue. Traveling at first by train to her many engagements, she eventually acquired an automobile. The meetings which in the beginning lasted almost a week were streamlined to occur in one day or less. As the work grew and more people were involved, some of the dearly held personal touches had to be sacrificed. Her own time seemed to shrink before her eyes as more and more demands were made upon it. And with every expanded program, the opportunity for personal, in-depth encounters seemed to reduce in direct proportion. With every gain there seemed to be some corresponding sacrifice to make, but it was an inevitable part of the larger work into which she had become so intricately woven. At last it had to end.

In 1961 she announced her retirement, effective at the end of the year. When the annual convention, her last as Woman's Missionary Union director for the state, met in Farmington, the women presented a wonderful tribute to her. In a garden setting, a pageant of her life unfolded beautifully. Various ladies brought flowers into the lovely bower, depicting different elements of her life of service, dedication, and consecration to her task. At the close, a small model of a ship was presented to her, bearing a gift from the women of the state who loved her so dearly. When she expressed her appreciation she used the time which normally would have been used for her annual report to extend a challenge to those gathered. And to her newly elected successor, Miss Vanita Baldwin of Florida, she left a message from the psalmist: "Teach me thy way, O Lord, and lead me in a plain path" (Ps. 27:11). It was the pathway she had sought for herself as leader of the women of the state for twenty-six years. She knew it to be the better way.

The 1961 annual of the Baptist Convention of New Mexico was dedicated to Miss Inlow that year. Under the lovely picture of Miss Inlow were inscribed these fitting words: "Founder and benefactor of Inlow Youth Camp. Twenty-six years of consecrated, dedicated service to New Mexico Baptists. Dean of Woman's Missionary Union Secretaries and major contributor to development of Woman's Missionary Union policies and programs of world missions."

Just before she left New Mexico, Miss Inlow drove once more to her beloved camp, high in the Manzano Mountains, for one last time. She walked down through the trees to a spot which has become sacred to hundreds of campers through the years—*Los Tres Pinos,* The Three Pines. It is a place of sublime beauty, a quiet place of meditation and prayer. There, once more, she dedicated the camp which bears her name to God, and prayed that it would never deviate from its original purpose, that all who came there would be refreshed and brought closer to their Creator and to his purpose for their lives.

Her prayers have been abundantly answered through the years, as the same high purposes on which the camp was established have been valiantly adhered to and as youth from across the state experience God's grace in their lives.

Miss Inlow left New Mexico and went on an extended trip touching mission lands around the world, and wherever she went she found missionaries serving in strategic places who had first dedicated themselves to God at Inlow Youth Camp. It was a thrill beyond compare to her, a kind of crown to her work, a benediction. It was a reassurance that all she had been about in her life had an eternal dimension.

Today Eva R. Inlow resides in a beautiful retirement home in the state of Washington. On the six floors of that building live two hundred and fifty people who range in age from sixty-five to one hundred and two years. Some of them are Christians while others are not. And so her ministry continues, as she believes with all her heart that she is there for a divine purpose. And although there may be a time for retirement from one's professional activity, she realizes keenly the truth that a Christian never retires from his duty and commitment to God, nor can he retire from the call of those who need him.

6.
More Than Money
R. Y. Bradford

Susan Key was a mere slip of a girl when she became the bride of John Bell Bradford. Her life seemed full of promise, opening to a wonderful future, as she waited for her young husband one noon. Suddenly, her whole body wrenched in a violent convulsion which would not release her, she lost consciousness, pitched forward, and fell heavily. She was alone. And her right hand rested in the burning fireplace.

No one could ever fully know the agony which must have gripped the soul of John Bradford when he found her there. Somehow, through his torture he was able to get Susan to medical care. When she awoke, her right hand and the lower half of her arm had been amputated. One month later she gave birth to her first child. She was eighteen years old.

The trauma of her loss haunted her, robbing her of peace, spiriting away her tranquility. She wept endless hours from the depths of her sorrow. Her mind reeled at her tragic loss. Its enormity was overwhelming. It was irreparable, incomprehensible. Nor did it yield to her importunity. And day after endless day, her heart almost breaking, she awoke from her troubled sleep to find that it was not a taunting dream.

Gradually, a change began to work its way into her heart and attitude. It was a quiet acceptance, a gentle acquiescence. There was nothing she could do to change the unchangeable. She had a husband she loved and a baby who needed her care. As best as she could she would overcome her loss. She must not sacrifice that which remained on the altar of that which was lost!

During the next years other children were added to the family until there were eleven. She sewed for her daughters as well as for her neighbors. She cooked, cleaned, baked pies and cakes, entertained guests, and was a member of the missionary society in her church. So adept was she in making up for her loss that her children never thought of it at all unless guests were present.

Into this home a son was born whom they named R. Y. When he was still very young his father heard that there was excellent farmland opening up near Rolf, Oklahoma. It was said to be especially suitable for the raising of corn.

Mr. Bradford loaded supplies and his family onto covered wagons and left his Ford County home near Crowell, Texas. They cooked and camped out along the way, taking a whole week to travel the almost two hundred miles. When they set up camp at night Mrs. Bradford cooked over the open campfire. Biscuits cooked in a skillet, cured pork sizzling over the fire, fried eggs, and potatoes had never been more tempting!

One evening a black man camped nearby and visited with them. The young lad remembers vividly his father's conversation with the man he called "Uncle." At night the children and their mother slept snugly in the wagons while their father maintained a watch outside. It was an exciting, unforgettable trip.

The Bradford children were enrolled in the Blue Mound, Oklahoma, school. It was a one room, one teacher school. They walked two-and-one-half miles each way, taking turns carrying their community lunch in a syrup bucket. Packed by their mother, the lunch contained nourishing food: a fried egg or a sausage inside a homemade biscuit. Often they opened their pail to find fried peach or apple pies, made skillfully by their mother. When he was old enough, R. Y. joined his siblings in this daily trek for learning.

He found himself placed in a double seat beside an Indian boy twice his size. His desk formed the seat for the students in front of them. The floors were bare and the wood stove was pressed into duty on cold wintry days. Blackboards filled the walls and erasers rested in their trays. Some of the children used slates for their lessons, but his mother bought narrow Big Chief tablets and twenty-five pencils at a time for her growing brood. At a penny each, it wasn't too great an outlay, but there was method in her purchase of the narrow paper tablets over the wide. If the children ruined a sheet, or didn't need as large a page, less paper was wasted!

The children were expected to recite about twice each day. They were to give forth that which they had learned the day before. And they were taught not to whisper.

In the evening there were the usual farm chores to be done. Water was brought in as well as kindling for the stove. Everyone took his turn doing the dishes after the evening meal.

After about four years in Oklahoma, where the promise of excellent crop failed to materialize, the Bradfords returned to Margaret, Texas, their original home. Settling once more into familiar surroundings, they quickly became part of the community and church life again.

John Bradford subscribed to a weekly paper, a forerunner of the *Dallas*

Morning News, and to another weekly publication, *Farm and Ranch.* His children heard him discuss the crops, the livestock, the weather, the health and well-being of family and friends, and Christian doctrine! There was no radio or television to bid for their time and when they had guests or when the pastor or evangelist came to dinner, the men always retired to the shade trees in front of their house or to the living room if the weather didn't permit. And by the hour they discussed the Scriptures and the great doctrines of the Bible. Young R. Y. sat in rapt attention, drinking in every word, and unwittingly acquiring a strong foundation of belief through this learning procedure.

Since the Baptist and Methodist churches were about the only denominations represented in that community, such subjects as the security of the believer, the mode and motive of baptism, and missions were prime targets. There were still those who felt there was no need whatever to send missionaries, questioning whether some nationalities even had a soul! (Interestingly, he never heard of the millennial question until he was a student in college.)

Thus, at a relatively early age, R. Y. Bradford had absorbed enough Bible knowledge that he strongly realized that he was lost, that there was a hell, that as a sinner he must be saved. He knew what was meant when the preacher mentioned "trusting Christ," and he fully believed with his mind every word that he heard. Listening to his father and the ministers talking hour after hour had sown conviction in his heart. Often, as he was in the fields alone, he felt a great sense of his need for God.

During a revival meeting (conducted each year, beginning on the Friday before the second Sunday in August), the pastor's wife, Mrs. J. B. McCrory, approached him and told him that she had been praying for him, that she wanted him to be saved. Her words of concern and interest gave him courage to do what he already wanted to do, but he felt it would be much easier if his friends were not around! He stepped into the aisle during the invitation and such a flood of emotion and joy overcame him that he wept with the thrill and release of it all. When he reached the pastor he told him that he wanted to give his heart to Jesus Christ. Although his was the only public decision registered that Monday morning, there were several others before the end of the meeting. He, along with eight other candidates, was baptized the following Sunday afternoon in a small concrete tank on his father's farm. Surprisingly during the week, he prayed audibly during a pre-service prayer meeting thanking God for his salvation.

It became his habit to read his New Testament and then to make his way into the fields after dark to pray. So absorbed was he in his new found life that he completed the first reading very quickly. Never has he forgotten the power which he received in his life from that initial diligent reading of the New Testament.

Before long he had an urgent sense of God's dealing with him. There was a growing awareness that God wanted him to preach. It was a continuously expanding thing. No one ever discussed it with him, but the year after his conversion he approached his pastor and told him of his impressions. The pastor was overjoyed and no doubt changed the subject of his next sermon in an attempt to meet his young parishioner's needs. He preached concerning the will of God and when he extended an invitation, R. Y. made his commitment public.

After completing the tenth grade at Margaret, his father borrowed $150 against his imminent cotton crop, took his son to Wayland Baptist Academy, moved him into a room on Kokomo Street with the help of another son, and thus made possible his continuing education for the ministry. Twenty-five dollars a month was required for board and room. He dug into his schoolwork and finished high school in the spring of 1926.

During those spring days of 1926 he was called as pastor of his first church. He had been licensed to preach by his home church. But the matter of ordination had to be attended to before he began his hitchhiking jaunts to meet his appointment each month for his one-fourth time pastorate at nearby Campbell.

It was customary in those days to have extended services as each fifth Sunday approached. Several churches were involved, as they started on Friday evening and continued through Sunday night. Fourteen or fifteen doctrinal messages were delivered, as the well-prepared ministers expounded great Bible truths. Since ordination services in that era were for the education and information of the congregation as well as for the intense questioning of the candidate, such an addition to their usual program could be made quite easily. There was great concern whether the man seeking ordination was really basic and fundamental in his denominational position. It was a most serious matter. Such a time was set aside for the eighteen-year-old Bradford, and he passed the test with flying colors. His own study, plus the hours spent listening to his father and others discussing the Scriptures, served him well.

That fall found him back on his father's farm. Mr. Bradford had become ill and needed his son to gather the fall crop and to plant and gather the crops the following spring. Until his father's death in September, 1927, R. Y. dutifully cared for his father's every interest. Thus his enrollment for college work was necessarily delayed a few weeks in the fall of that year.

Ila Wright, enrolling for college classes after her graduation from Wayland Academy the previous summer, noted a flurry of activity near one of the teachers registering pupils for the new semester. At the center of the circle stood a tall slender youth, greeting friends from many months before. Perfectly groomed, his hair was a rich sorrel color and framed his face with natural waves. She thought R. Y. to be exceptionally handsome.

One of the most popular activities on campus involved the Volunteer Mission Band. The students who were members of that organization went to various churches in the surrounding areas where they conducted services and participated as their various talents allowed. When R. Y. was not preaching, he often accompanied this group and gained much practical experience. At one such service Ila Wright, from Floydada, Texas, gave her testimony. He was deeply impressed by her sincerity, but he had interests back home.

When the students visited the churches they traveled by bus. The driver was often an older student, Jack DeVore, who later served as a pastor in New Mexico with distinction. On a trip to Dallas to attend the Baptist Student Union Convention their route took them through Crowell, near R. Y.'s hometown. When the bus stopped and the students alighted for breakfast,

R. Y. and a friend took the few short minutes to make a hurried trip to see their girlfriends in Margaret. They missed breakfast, but it was worth it!

On Valentine's Day a box of candy was bought with the hometown girl in mind. However, in a moment of great insight, he presented the gift to Ila Wright! His impression of her over a period of time was consistently good. He was strongly attracted to her. Their mutual extracurricular activities at the college had given him frequent opportunities to observe her worth. Reared in the First Baptist Church of Floydada, her father ran the town's country store. She was from a solid family background, she was intelligent, and a dedicated Christian. And she accepted the candy!

Immediately their trips were modified. No longer could they travel together on the same bus to appear on the same church programs. It was an unalterable rule that when two students began to be romantically involved with each other, trips were no longer made concurrently.

However, by January of 1929 the two were formally engaged. And the next month he was called as pastor of the First Baptist Church of Stinnett, in the Panhandle of Texas. He moved there alone, but on August 6 he claimed his bride and they moved into their home together.

This home was three rooms in the church building, which had formerly served as the courthouse. Over one of their rooms a sign read "Sheriff's Office," while another announced "Clerk's Office!" The walls were unpainted and there were no locks on any doors. Water was bought in barrels at fifty cents each and when dinners were served at the church, their kitchen was appropriated. But they were happy. And they were doing what they felt called to do.

Ila began to teach school in Stinnett. She kept her house and taught a Sunday School class while her young husband began to do everything he could to build the church. In those days Stinnett was a "boom" town and people of every stratum of life came from everywhere to claim their stake in the oil business. Law and order became increasingly difficult to maintain with this melting pot of humanity—many of whom didn't "melt." Robbery, corruption, drinking, and political graft increased to the point that the state was forced to assume control. A state of martial law was declared and the Texas officials moved in, their very presence seeming to deter the increasing crime.

One night, however, there was a jailbreak. People sought places of refuge and the church was one such refuge! The fact that no locks were on the doors made the Bradfords realize that they should seek another place of security.

They remembered that one night someone had slipped into one of the Sunday School rooms to spend the night, and another time a family camped in front of the church.

Some years before R. Y. had listened intently to a missionary from China. As he sat in his home church, drinking in every word, the message made a tremendous impression on him. During his years in Wayland College there was a great deal of emphasis on missions. The environment on that campus was distinctly Christian and his heart was bathed in rich fellowship as his soul seemed to grow during those days. He began to wonder whether God might use him as a missionary and this haunting awareness began to grow and trouble him.

As he tried to determine God's definitive will for his life he left his room one night and walked out to a little cotton patch where he talked it over with God. He told God that he wanted to do his will completely and that he would go to the ends of the earth if that was where God wanted him to serve.

Perhaps no audible voice from God was heard, but in as powerful a manner as God manifests himself to mortal man, R. Y. knew that God was saying, "I didn't want you to go to China, I wanted you to be willing to go!" This mighty awareness of God's leadership, coupled with his commitment to be a pliable servant, gave him a concern and bent toward missions which he might not otherwise have had.

After four years in Stinnett, the Bradfords felt that R. Y. must complete his education. But leaving the church was a traumatic experience for them. They had become attached to the people in such a way that even today they say, "When we think of them there is a deep feeling of friendship, stronger than that of pastor and people." And Dr. Bradford adds, "If I had my choice I would pastor people connected with the oil fields. They are loyal, generous, and have big hearts. They have almost a pioneering spirit. I emphasized tithing during our years in Stinnett and every adult member was a tither! And that continued on after we left."

Mrs. Bradford resigned her teaching position and they bundled up their tiny daughter and moved to Shawnee, Oklahoma. They found an apartment (with garage) for $7.50 a month and during their entire stay at Oklahoma Baptist University the rent was never raised. Their duplex neighbors were a joy to them. Young Jesse Northcutt was also a student at OBU and he and Mrs. Northcutt have remained treasured friends. (Dr. Northcutt has served as a distinguished professor at Southwestern Baptist Theological Seminary in Fort Worth, Texas, for many years.)

Soon R. Y. was called to pastor halftime churches at Rolf and Milburn, Oklahoma. He served these churches throughout his college days and on enrollment at the Fort Worth Seminary commuted by train for a time.

In September 1935, the Bradfords moved to Fort Worth, while the young minister continued his studies. He sat under the instruction of veritable giants: Dr. H. E. Dana, Dr. W. T. Conner, Dr. W. W. Barnes, Dr. T. B. Maston, Dr. Jeff D. Ray, Dr. B. A. Copass, and Dr. Baker James Cauthen, as well as Dr. J. M. Price. It was a time of wonderful life enrichment, of learning, and motivation. One can never completely get away from such depths of training. It permeates one's ministry until the end of life.

When R. Y. Bradford completed his seminary training in the spring of 1938, he was awarded the degree of Master of Theology. He had waded through Greek and Hebrew, Old Testament and New Testament. He had delved into theology, evangelism, and social ethics. He had studied church history, archaelogy, comparative religion, and homiletics. Other courses added to this curriculum served to give him a balanced and overall knowledge which he drew from for the rest of his days.

Upon graduation he accepted the pastorate of nearby Grandview, Texas. By this time three children were a vital part of their lives and Mrs. Bradford gave her full time to being a mother to them, a wife and homemaker for her busy husband, and pastor's wife to their growing church. Calm and unflappable in manner, she was a constant strength and help wherever she functioned. Countless times her husband was to hear the phrase "a perfect pastor's wife," as descriptive of his loyal companion.

The threat of war was in the air. In Europe, the news grew worse each day. The valiant attempt of the United States to avert her own involvement was short-lived. Soon the call began to go out for volunteers, for soldiers, for builders of weapons and planes, for dentists and doctors, and for chaplains.

Each denomination in the country was requested to furnish a certain quota of ministers, based on its membership. Although certainly not a mandatory ruling, it was a matter of honor, of patriotism. And growing in the heart of Grandview's pastor was the awareness that he was fully equipped to serve his country in such a spiritual capacity. He first went into the reserve forces and then was called for active duty in early 1941. Assigned to Albuquerque Army Air Force Base (now Kirtland Field), he moved his family to that New Mexico city in April, thus becoming the first military chaplain when the base opened. In September of the following year he was assigned to the Ninth Air Force, being activated at Patterson Field, Ohio. He was one of the first officers of the

Ninth Air Force Service Command, and was assigned as command chaplain. Mrs. Bradford returned to Floydada, where her parents still lived, bought a home, and cared for their children while her husband was serving overseas. At such a time, who can be called the more valiant, the one who goes or the one who stays? And for whom is the time longer or the victory sweeter? For whom can letters exchanged across the seas be more meaningful, or the day of return more blessed? For whom can the dangers be more real and the trauma of separation more poignant? For whom, indeed!

When Chaplain Bradford was first assigned to duty he was given the rank of first lieutenant. He rose quickly through the following months as he was promoted to captain in 1942, major in 1943, and lieutenant colonel the following year. He had from the first, however, served on the level of a lieutenant colonel because of the position he held as command chaplain.

He was sent to the Middle East, to Tripoli, and Cairo where the Ninth Air Force supported the British forces in driving Rommel out of Egypt. Field Marshall Erwin Rommel, one of the most brilliant generals of World War II, commanded the Afrika Korps. His clever tactics earned for him the name "The Desert Fox" but he later lost his command in Normandy when he opposed his commander-in-chief, Adolph Hitler. In late 1942 he was forced out of Africa by the Allies.

Reaching Cairo just before Christmas, the new command chaplain was asked to deliver the Christmas message for all the troops who would come. He chose as his subject to deliver to that heterogeneous group "The By-Products of Christianity." He contrasted the non-Christian country of Egypt with the blessings enjoyed in America because of the Christian ethic and philosophy. He listed as by-products such benefits as the Christian home, the elevation of womanhood, the liberties of the individual and the freedom of worship.

En route he had preached aboard ship as they crossed the Atlantic and Indian Oceans. He journeyed to the various bases on the Libyan Desert and preached at each stop. He tried in his messages to stay away from the dangers which they faced on the fighting field. He felt that such motivation was not the best reason for one's relation to God, and dwelt more on God's love and care. He never felt constricted at all in his topics or their development, but used his own good judgment to give support and encouragement and hope in that busy theater of war. In almost every message he dealt with an evangelistic theme. Such men, facing death, needed most of all to be made aware of the message of salvation.

As a general rule, headquarters were located in Cairo, although the fighting troops were north of that locale. King Farouk was holding forth in lavish splendor as the last monarch of Egypt. During the days of the US occupation in Egypt, news of Farouk's wanton and profligate life made headlines around the world. It was during this period that he divorced his wife because she had not presented him with a male heir to the throne. He had only three daughters! And the world watched with wonder as he took another bride. He was forced into exile in 1952. The monarchy in Egypt was at an end.

Colonel Bradford's unit was a service unit. Almost one-half the men in the Ninth Air Force (about 100,000 men) were in the Service Command. He dealt with large problems involving the lives and morale of masses of people.

About five times each week staff meetings were held where the commanding general, his Executive officer, the adjutant general, the planning division, the operational division and the command chaplain were present. The group was briefed on confidential information having to do with the war, especially as it related to Air Force activities.

In addition to the conducting of regular religious services, the chaplains served as liaison between the soldier and his family, as such need arose. Chaplain Bradford carefully screened all letters written to families by other chaplains of the Ninth Air Force Service Command. Such letters were sent at the time of a soldier's death and Chaplain Bradford made certain that no gruesome details were unnecessarily added to augment their grief. He also checked letters written to families of men listed as missing in action to ensure that false hopes were not aroused and yet that nothing was said which would destroy such hopes. (Unit commanders screened letters to assure that no confidential information was leaked.)

Also, the chaplains represented their men before the commanding general, in certain cases, and also served as a link with the community. Certain problems arose which needed prompt solution and often the chaplains worked with the local priests or ministers if a civilian became involved with an American service man. As command chaplain, Colonel Bradford also was the point of reference for the individual ministers as well. They too had problems which he tried to improve. It was a full time, albeit rewarding, job!

In October of 1943, Colonel Bradford and his command were transferred to Europe. During the next months he was to see duty in England, France, Luxembourg, and at the Advance Headquarters in Germany. He saw General Dwight David Eisenhower in Paris and was present when the Eternal Flame was again lighted after extinction by the German Army during its occupation. The French, British, and Americans were present as the mayor of Paris approached the Arc de Triomphe on the Champs Élysées and lighted the torch at the tomb of France's Unknown Soldier where twelve avenues meet. It was symbolic of hope and continuing freedom, for a moment in time extinguished by an alien foe.

Toward the end of the war it fell Chaplain Bradford's lot to determine which chaplains would come home, who would remain in the occupied territory in Europe, and who would be sent for action in the South Pacific! It was an awesome task and fraught with emotional overtones. Further, it was possible that such assignments would make a difference between life and death.

At last he took a detailed list of the chaplains under his supervision. He ranked each according to the length of time he had been overseas. Those who had been away the longest were assigned to units which would be going home first; those who had been in Europe (or overseas) for the shortest period of time would be assigned to units en route to the Pacific. And those in between would remain in Europe with our occupational forces. Not one chaplain complained to him or asked him for a reappraisal! Each seemed to realize the brilliance and fairness of the decision as well as the difficulty faced. Some of the men had been away from home for thirty months, their command chaplain had been gone thirty-five!

Chaplain Bradford was the fourth officer from a total of over 200,000 men to be returned home. The decision was made on points relative to length of time overseas, time in service, campaign stars, and family. It was a heady day when he boarded an old war-weary B-17, bandaged together after having been shot down during the war. Its pilot had somehow managed to fly the plane into neutral Switzerland where the craft was "scotch-taped" together. And now it was being flown back to the States for propaganda purposes. There were no seats aboard. The men simply threw their parachutes down in the plane and used them as cushions.

No doubt, there were many crowding thoughts vying for his attention as he flew homeward. He was proud of his denomination, as Southern Baptists had more than fulfilled their quota of requested chaplains, and had served with honor. He was grateful for the opportunity to serve his country in a time of great crisis and to be a witness for his God. He remembered his valiant wife who had coped through the long months of separation with such inconvenience as gas rationing and food stamps; endured the childhood mishaps (such as a broken leg which their son suffered), but who was a part of the life of her church in Floydada. Their two youngest children had been baptized during his absence and their oldest was entering high school. It was not the same family to which he was returning as far as weight, stature, and achievement were concerned, but in all the ways that mattered, it was the same! He remembered that a month would often pass before he was aware of any crisis at home due to the slowness of the mail. He had simply turned his family over to God to take care of them. There was no more that he could do. But the knowledge that God was with them had made it possible for him to function with an undivided mind.

Mrs. Bradford took her family to church faithfully, where they sat under the capable leadership of Reverend L. A. Doyle (who later served as pastor of the First Baptist Church of Portales, New Mexico, for many years). It was during this time in Floydada that the church began to experience unusual growth under their pastor's strong and capable leadership. The Bradford family was always grateful for such spritual strength during those times of stress. And August, 1945, brought them joyfully back together once again.

After his separation from the service, following three or four months of accumulated leave, he and Mrs. Bradford attended the Texas Baptist Convention in Fort Worth. Dr. W. W. Melton was completing his tenure as executive secretary of the Baptist General Convention of Texas and it was a memorable year. Too, there were many wonderful reunions as friends were greeted.

He was home again!

When he went to Colorado City to preach for that pastorless church he found to his surprise that his name had been acquired from another church who was also without a pastor! He was invited for another Sunday, whereupon the church promptly called him as their pastor. And he accepted.

Moving to Colorado City he discovered that the church's budget was approximately $16,000 a year. Although he had never preached a full stewardship sermon, stewardship and missions penetrated each one. The church had been giving less than $200 each year for the Lottie Moon Christmas Offering. As soon as he could judiciously do so, he suggested that twenty-five families might be challenged to give $100 each to the special offering. That year their total Christmas gifts were $4,700! The next year he asked one hundred families to give twenty-five dollars each. An excess of $6,700 was given! The people were proud and grateful for their new plateau of missions commitment and the year the Bradfords left the church a total of $21,000 was given to mission causes alone! And never has the level of stewardship been permitted to falter in the intervening years.

In gifts through the Cooperative Program, the pastor led them to raise that item from $3,600 to $10,000 in one jump! R. Y. Bradford believes strongly that a church must be just as diligent and accountable in the handling of its funds in order to give to world missions as the church expects its members to be! "I've been convinced for thirty years," he stated, "that the Cooperative Program is the lifeline of all our programs and without it we'd have no undergirding for the work which is being done by our special offerings. It is a comingling of funds. A missions dollar is a missions dollar. We sometimes say that the Lottie Moon Offering goes in toto to missions causes . . . but we must never lose sight of the fact that those dollars go to work that is being supported all year long by our Cooperative dollars! Without those Cooperative gifts there would be no place to send our Lottie Moon dollars." He further believes that giving to a specific cause on any field around the world is missions, but that buying a Sunday School quarterly for a child is, too!

In 1952, Texas Baptists initiated a program for Western missions. It marked the beginning of the loan fund established by Texas Baptists. And Mr. Bradford led the church he pastored to give $3,500 to this cause. They were elated and grateful because their gift was so worthy in proportion to the size of their membership. "But in my rejoicing," the minister recalls, "the Lord said to me: 'It takes more than money to do work in the West' . . . I immediately realized that God was saying something to me about my life. In my private devotion I said, "Lord, if you want me to go out West, I'll go.' "

Mr. Bradford attended the executive board meeting for Texas Baptists shortly afterward. When he returned from Dallas his wife told him of a telephone call he had received while he was away, from Santa Fe, New Mexico. The call would be returned the following day. And immediately R. Y. Bradford remembered his promise to God: "If you want me to go out West, I'll go." He didn't know until that moment that the church in the nation's oldest capital city was without a pastor. Even so, he now had an overriding conviction that his life was about to take a much different direction. And he knew that he would return the telephone call.

When it came the next day the minister could in no way refuse the invitation to visit that city. It was, as the pastor had known it would be, the pulpit committee chairman from the First Baptist Church of Santa Fe.

The Bradfords had just moved into a spacious four bedroom home, completely carpeted, air conditioned, and with the other equipment associated with a home of that size. When he was shown the pastorium in Santa Fe it was a small house with two small bedrooms. The salary he was offered was one hundred dollars a month less than he was receiving. And while 471 had attended Sunday School in his Colorado City pastorate the previous Sunday, 131 appeared in Santa Fe. Nevertheless, when the church extended an invitation for him to become their pastor, there was never any question in his mind that God was leading in a very definite way. He accepted their call and moved his family into much smaller quarters. Although later the salary was adjusted and a larger home, more adequate for their needs, was provided, he had met God's challenge: "I want you to be willing!" And he was!

The church property was near the center of the city, a block from the state capitol building. However, there was virtually no parking space and no opportunity for expansion whatsoever. A committee began to look about for suitable land on which to build. They wanted at least four acres. Much of the available land had such stringent restrictions that the erection of a church was prohibitive, if not completely impossible. At last, the committee became aware of property left by Mr. Nat Sterne, on which there were no restrictions. The trustees of his estate were approached by the church group and were told, "If the church wants it, we won't offer it for sale." Thus, in 1956 they purchased 9.2 acres for $17,000, on a beautiful site overlooking Santa Fe and and on the main thoroughfare leading to the Glorieta Conference Center and Las Vegas. (Today—1977—the unofficial appraisal for the same property is $60,000 an acre!)

The church building fund had accumulated a sum of approximately $43,000. To their chagrin, however, they discovered that building materials seemed to rise in cost in direct proportion to their growing savings! They invited Mr. Eugene Brand, then with the A. B. Culbertson Company, to come to Santa Fe and help them in a drive to issue bonds in the amount of $100,000. That marked the first time in Santa Fe that church bonds had ever been issued. A number of non-Baptist business people purchased the bonds, feeling that they were a safe investment, and no doubt wanting to be a part of a worthy cause.

After the architect had drawn up the plans for the building the contracts were let. The lowest bid came in at $270,000! So, it was back to the drawing board. Certain embellishments were cut, but the basic structure was to remain the same. Furthermore, additional bonds in the amount of the original bond drive were sold and at last the contract was let. The total was for $275,000 which included the land, the architect's fees, plus the structure itself.

It is a totally unique building, blending into the rugged landscape of Santa Fe perfectly. No church building in the entire Southern Baptist Convention matches its style. It is Indian-Spanish in design, pueblo style. Resting on the highest point in the area, it was the first public building erected in that part of Santa Fe. Today a hospital is being constructed nearby and other churches and public buildings have been built in the vicinity. When the church building was dedicated on December 11, 1960, the *Santa Fe New Mexican* gave two pages of coverage to the new house of worship. On a par with any church building in the city, the appraisers rated it one of the finest structures in Santa Fe. As an added bonus, it did more to bring recognition and prestige to Baptist work in Santa Fe than anything done up to that time. Its presence is a vivid reminder of the sacrifice of those who were a part of its realization. The old property was sold for $60,000 and two-thirds that amount was applied to their debt, while the remainder was used for furnishings and other equipment for the new building.

For some time the budget committee set aside $500 each week for the liquidation of their loan. When the balance rested at $150,000 a banker agreed to loan them money so that the bonds could be paid immediately. And at 4½ percent interest! The bonds were then called in and paid. Within seven years of their dedication, the building was declared free of indebtedness! Paying their note three years ahead of schedule, of course, made their standing in the financial community extremely secure and respected.

His fourteen years as pastor in a city where the diversity of cultures is apparent everywhere, and where the Catholic Church is the dominant religious force, were nevertheless quite rewarding. He served as a member of the board of directors of St. Vincent Hospital and was often called by the nuns to assist in times of illness or emergency. He was a member of the advisory board of the New Mexico Fair Employment Commission where alleged discriminatory practices in the labor force were examined. In addition, he served on the State Mission Board of the Baptist Convention of New Mexico for two terms and was president of that body for two years.

In 1958 he was asked to preach the annual sermon for the state convention. He was named to serve on the Committee on Boards for the Southern Baptist Convention as well as the Southern Baptist Convention's Radio and Television Commission.

His adopted state had received him well and he was in demand for various types of speaking engagements, revivals, and other meetings. Twice he was approached in regard to positions with the Baptist Convention of New Mexico. But he felt led to remain in Santa Fe. He was a builder of churches. He never left a church, that wasn't in better condition in every way than when he had begun his work there. He worked hard, he was diligent in his pastoral ministry, he was an excellent student, and consequently, a thought-provoking preacher.

At the end of 1967 Dr. Harry P. Stagg, for thirty years the beloved executive secretary of the Baptist Convention of New Mexico, retired. After those years of tremendous expansion, so marked by his vision and personality, rumors flew thick and fast as attempts were made to guess who would be his successor. A member of the search committee approached R. Y. Bradford, and wanted permission to submit his name. (The committee was to consider no one whose name had not been formally presented.) When Mr. Bradford didn't respond, a deacon from the First Baptist Church of Santa Fe was asked to write a letter concerning his pastor. However, Mr. Bradford felt strongly that someone else would be selected.

In Raton for a revival meeting, his host pastor said one day, "Who do you suppose will succeed Dr. Stagg?"

Immediately, R. Y. Bradford suggested the name of a man he felt was foremost under consideration. And just as immediately he felt rebuked! The name almost choked in his throat. During those days away from home he had a growing impression that God wanted him in that position.

Returning to Santa Fe he said to his wife, "I have a fearful feeling that I am going to be elected executive secretary!"

Quietly she replied, "I have, too."

It was not a position to seek, nor was it one to covet. Neither was it one to dismiss lightly. Nor is any position in the kingdom of God. No man motivated by power or prestige or financial gain could possibly understand the various movings of the Holy Spirit as he prepares a willing, obedient servant for a work known only to God. He could not understand a man's sacrifices to attend school for endless years in order to acquire tools for better servitude, nor could he ever comprehend a man's leaving his family behind for several years to render a spiritual service in a war on two distant continents. He could never believe that there was not some unknown motive in a pastor's leaving a church for a lesser salary in a more difficult field and with fewer people to assist. It is only the seeking heart, touched by God, who can see the vision of what God can accomplish when his life is laid on the line of self-denial and submission—with no questions asked! And it is only that Christian whose life's direction is open to God who will find the most abundant life, the greatest realization of that which he was made by his Creator to do.

He was asked to come for an interview with the search committee. With his frame of mind and heart there was nothing for him to do but to accept their

110

invitation. He was one of three they held conferences with that day.

The next morning he was back in his familiar office. Mentally he awaited their call. He knew they would call, and they did! The committee recognized in him the man who was of the disposition and experience which uniquely fitted him as successor to the man who had led so effectively for nearly a third of a century. And he had no doubts at all. There was no question in his mind but that God had prepared him to accept that work.

During the next seven years Dr. Bradford continuously felt the leadership and the blessings of the Lord as he served as executive director for the Baptist Convention of New Mexico. Beginning his work in October of 1967 he learned the tasks which were to be his. He studied convention polity, the composition, and function of the staff. He informed himself as to the financial structure and the myriad interests of the children's home in Portales and the two state camps. He was advised of the involvements of the five Baptist Student Unions and learned the relationship of the home missionaries to the missions' director. He eased into his involvements with executive directors from states all over the Convention territory and began to serve as liaison with the many various Southern Baptist Convention agencies. Under the instruction of Dr. Stagg, he was gradually oriented in the duties he was to assume. He already knew much of the working of the board and the convention he was to serve, but on the other side of the desk, there was more to familiarize himself with.

Meanwhile, his calendar was filling to the brim, his appointments were tumbling over each other, and the mail came twice a day. It was opened, stamped with the date received, and placed on his desk in three tidy stacks: "Urgent—Pressing—Can wait an hour!" It was a full time position!

In 1970, after careful study, the staff of the convention was completely restructured. Attention was also given to building an operational reserve as well as a fund for special missions projects. Programs previously begun were expanded and more heavily undergirded. He represented New Mexico Baptists at countless meetings and traveled the state constantly in his ministry to them. In everything he did, his main motive was what it had always been—to be a builder of churches.

Somehow he made time to serve as a trustee on the Board of Health, Education, and Livelihood Program. This organization was designed to help people to become more self-sufficient. Conducted entirely in Spanish, earphones were provided during the sessions for those members who were not bilingual.

Seven years passed very rapidly and Dr. Bradford knew that only too well. As he approached retirement, he felt that he still had considerable vigor and health and he certainly had the urgent desire to be of service.

Six months before he was to retire from his position with the Baptist Convention of New Mexico, he met with the officials of Strong-Thorne Mortuary, a firm which conducts over one thousand funerals a year. He was told that he could set his own hours as chaplain for their concern and fulfill the needs of the families as he saw fit. Since many people in a city the size of Albuquerque do not have a minister of their own, the presence of a chaplain on the Strong-Thorne staff seemed most beneficial. And Dr. Bradford was well prepared for pioneering in this new endeavor.

The transition was smooth and conducted in an orderly fashion. When Dr. Bradford's successor was chosen and moved to Albuquerque, he quietly moved from his spacious office to a small room across the hall. And he gave his full time to the new executive director.

He made himself available on a moment's notice to help the new administrator to become as quickly informed and oriented as possible. He had, by request, previously arranged for the staff to interview with their new leader. As much as one mortal man can help another, he became indispensable to the new arrival during the transitional period. For two weeks he delayed his own plans and in February accompanied his confrere to Nashville and Mobile for the annual meetings of the executive directors and editors of the Southern Baptist Convention. He graciously presented his state's new executive to his peers and the extended courtesy was so remarkable and unprecedented that the group felt such a formal passage should be made standard procedure.

In addition, he has been of inestimable value as a friend, as a counselor, and as a wonderful supporter of the man who now occupies his former office.

On leaving the Baptist Building, Dr. Bradford moved only a few blocks away to an entirely new and greatly needed ministry. He makes contact with every family involved with the mortuary and attempts to minister to their individual needs. He counsels with them during their sorrow and has prayer with them. Often his prayer is the only one they hear during their period of mourning; it may be the only one they have listened to in years! Often he officies during the service itself. He always makes a cassette tape of the funeral service. He carefully screens each tape to make certain there are no excesses of emotion, which might make the families and friends more intense. Several days after the memorial service, he telephones the family for an appointment, visits them once more, and presents the cassette to them.

During his initial visitation with a family, he is often able to answer questions concerning the professional services of the mortuary. And he also discusses the fact that God is able to help them through their sorrow. He often presents the reality of death and its finality as it relates to the mortal body. He discusses the normality of sorrow and assures them that it should be expressed in the manner conforming to each individual's personality. Not only should sorrow not be inhibited, it should not master one! To widows, especially, he advises them not to reach the place where they "enjoy" their sorrow, and not to let it control their lives. This can often occur when undue attention is focused on them for too long a period. Thus many are often reluctant to give up the condition (grief) which brought the intense notice and solicitude beamed in their direction. He urges them to live normal, active lives, and makes follow-up calls to determine whether they might serve in some volunteer capacity to help others, such as the Meals-on-Wheels program or as a candy striper in a hospital, or other such assistance. He tries to be prepared to serve every need imaginable, to individualize his ministry to fit the person or family involved.

In the twenty-two months of his chaplaincy at Strong-Thorne, he has personally conducted one hundred and forty-one funeral services. (But he is involved in virtually every one—ushering, driving the family car, etc.)

Preparing for such diverse funeral messages has proved to be quite a challenge. But God has given him some unusual messages. He feels strongly that the service should be Christian, but that evangelism should not be pressed upon the bewildered listeners. Nor should it be a time to establish Christian doctrine. It is a time to relate to the family, if possible, to suffer with them, and to honor Christ in it all.

Most of the services he conducts are for people whom he has never seen before. Sometimes he goes into the room where the body is lying and studies the individual very carefully. Often something of the person's character is revealed, and he thus has a point of reference.

One night he retired, knowing full well that the funeral message he was to deliver the next day was in some elusive state. It had to be! He certainly didn't have it in mind. It nagged at him during the night and about three o'clock the following morning he arose and opened Mrs. Edith Deen's book, *All of the Women of the Bible*. He turned to her treatment of Abigail. Scripture describes Abigail as one who was of "fair countenance and good understanding." He developed the message with the theme that Abigail was a woman who was at her best when others were at their worst. Unknown to Dr. Bradford, the deceased had two sons who were alcoholics as her late husband had been. She had lived with one of the sons, until her death, brief hours ago, at the advanced age of ninety-two years. But even so, she cared for her son. She was at her best when he was at his worst! In his message of comfort Dr. Bradford touched on these gracious qualities and discussed intercessory concern, faith in God, independent of circumstances. Later a daughter-in-law said, "God had to give you that message! " It had so beautifully fitted the occasion and the life of the dead lady that her daughter-in-law knew instinctively the source of its inspiration.

When a lady from Lebanon died, he told the story of the Shunammite woman and her gracious hospitality to the servant of God, Elisha. Gehazi commended the woman on Elisha's behalf and asked whether he and his master might reward her in some manner, such as being mentioned to the king or the captain of the hosts. But she replied simply, "I dwell among my own people." Dr. Bradford used this beautiful story to show how the hospitable woman did her splendid deeds not to impress others, but because of the loveliness of her own character. She would not accept favors which would compromise her own individuality. She had a direct approach to God. The family of the deceased was delighted with the message as they told him, "If you had known her all her life you could not have better described our mother!"

Often there are those who are very angry because of what has happened. They are sometimes vocally abusive in their resentment as they question: "Why did God do that to me?" At such times the chaplain wisely answers, "We don't know why." God has a permissive will. He permits his natural laws to remain inviolate as a rule. He set them in motion and seldom is known to intervene. When we violate them, there is a penalty, a consequence. He assures them that God can control and that what occurred may not necessarily be a result of God's causative will.

Sometimes the anger is directed at Dr. Bradford himself. He is the one present, a likely target. One day a woman appeared in his office and seemed to set the whole atmosphere aboiling. She knew that he was to preach the sermon for her daughter's funeral. But she informed him abusively: "My daughter didn't believe in God; I don't believe in God; my daughter didn't go to church; I don't go to church; my daughter didn't believe in a hereafter; I don't believe in a hereafter!" And on and on, ad infinitum.

When she was spent of her emotional fury, Dr. Bradford replied, gently and quietly, "What you don't believe doesn't keep God from loving you and what you don't believe doesn't keep me from caring that you are hurt!"

The woman was completely disarmed and the conversation helped to settle her raging sorrow and her angry grief.

On the wall of Dr. Bradford's office are several treasured mementos, reflective of his life's energies and pursuits. His framed diploma from Oklahoma Baptist University hangs there as well as the diploma from Southwestern Baptist Theological Seminary, signed by Dr. George W. Truett and Dr. L. R. Scarborough. The honorary doctoral certificate conferred by Wayland College in 1970, is there. The plaque presented at the close of his years as executive director, and signed by Dr. Porter Routh, is there in silent tribute. Nearby hangs a certificate from the Radio and TV Commission in recognition of valued service rendered.

He holds the honorary colonel aide-de-camp from former New Mexico Governor Bruce King, and is listed in *Who's Who in the West, Who's Who in Religion,* and in *Who's Who Honorary Society of America.* One of the most poignant plaques was presented in the city of Luxembourg by General Wood, and along with a gracious citation begins:

IX Air Force Service Command . . . The Bronze Star Medal . . . (he) organized and supervised the spiritual activities of the Command in an exemplary and exceptional manner. June 4, 1945.
Myron R. Wood, Brigadier General, USA-Commanding . . .

When in military uniform Colonel Bradford is entitled to wear seven campaign stars, the Presidential citation, plus a multitude of ribbons earned in the service to his country. He has served well: pastor, chaplain, executive director, and chaplain.

In looking over the life of R. Y. Bradford one cannot but be impressed with his devotion to God, to his country, to his family, to his church, and to each phase of a remarkable career. Encompassing the days of his life, as he sought to follow God's leadership each step of the way, one remembers the haunting words he felt God speak to his heart which led him West: "It takes more than money . . ."

Although he led churches in stewardship for the purpose of extending missions and building buildings, although he led New Mexico Baptists in a financially strong stance, and though he himself was prudent in the expenditure of his own funds, and gave through the church on a sacrificial basis, he gave more. That was what was required of him. And that was what he gave. *More than money!*

7.
To Share the Victory
José Rey Toledo

Nestled on the shelf of a mountain which slopes into the valley toward a slender thread of river is the Jemez Pueblo. The Indian village is dwarfed by the magnificent mountains which bear its name and is hard by an ancient volcanic *caldera,* a basin formed eons ago when the surface collapsed, leaving volcanic ash and lava for a stretch of four hundred square miles. In the interim, the erosive forces of water and wind carved the starkly beautiful canyons and mesas. Eventually, a vast forest covered the land, except for a scattering of bare spots on the hillsides and the age-old meadows in the valley.

Antiquity hangs heavily in the pueblo when one remembers that the land, long inhabited by the Indians, was granted to them in 1689, ''by the grace of Spain.'' However, their more distant ancestral sites reached deep into the huge forest.

Encouraged by the Spanish, they set about selecting a governor each year. They were aided in this procedure by their *cacique,* the religious leader who served for life. An Arawakan word from the Caribbean, *cacique* simply means ''chief'' and he is a vital part of pueblo life until this day.

Councils were held with their governor presiding. Time was unimportant. The major desire was to reach unanimity of agreement if possible. This was important in the pueblos.

The Spanish governor gave each pueblo governor a silver-headed cane, an agreeable badge of office. And when, in 1863, twenty pueblo governors visited President Lincoln, he presented them with canes with his name and the date inscribed upon them. These two canes must be in possession of the governor before he is deemed fully installed and empowered to act.

Even with these additions to their way of life and the intrusion of other religious teachings, little was changed in the deep currents of their existence. Group solidarity was maintained and through this method strength was achieved for the individual. In turn, each person was always expected to act with the larger group—or clan—in mind.

Eight miles from the Jemez as the crow flies one comes to the Zia Pueblo,

chronicled by Castañeda in his report of the Coronado expedition in 1540. Life at Zia strongly resembles that of its neighboring Jemez.

One can visualize a tiny youth following his feet toward the Zia Pueblo where a dear grandmother lived. Tenderly she cared for him, her love reaching out to him in a thousand ways. When he arose in the morning she was working at the fireplace, cooking their meal. The mattresses on which they had slept were rolled against the wall to form benches during the day. As he sat on the adobe floor his grandmother served the food, but not until they paused to recognize the guiding spirit for their existence and to express gratitude for their food. Perhaps gratitude was the first emotion taught the child. It was a built-in influence as he learned to remember the spirit and to pay tribute to him. It was very important that they were aware of something above themselves. As they observed these influences in the fire, in their food, in the running rivers and streams, and in the magnificent mountains and rolling plains, they were to reflect on this guiding spirit and to become aware that they owed allegiance to this undefined spiritual value which men invariably seek.

In the simple life they lived, the children were taught to eat with dignity. They were not to rush. They were not to laugh. They were to pay attention to the formality of eating, because they were nourishing their bodies. They could talk, but not unnecessarily. And as the grandmother imparted these noble values, she did so in an intimate manner by her own worthy example.

Back in his own pueblo, the small boy observed many other things as he grew toward manhood. He watched the cultivation and the gathering of the crops as pumpkins, squash, chilies, cotton, and tobacco, were coaxed from the ground. He saw the horses. He watched the care of the cattle and sheep and learned that they furnished food and wool for clothing and leather for his moccasins. He saw that the tobacco and cotton were used in ceremonies during religious observances. He saw men leave for the hunt and return with their kill. And he watched as his father bartered with the traders for farm implements or agricultural products or clothing. They, in turn, left with valuable fur pelts or hundred pound sacks of corn. He could not understand at that youthful age that these traders were from faraway Syria and Lebanon, that some were German-Jews. Nearly all of them were seeking to establish their citizenship in the United States as they bartered on the frontiers of the country.

He ate the nourishing food, the mutton, the beef, and the game. He enjoyed the delicious bread baked outside in the *horno,* and he enjoyed the farm staples from their lands. Poured into every fiber of his being was the rich heritage of his Hope-Zia mother and father who embodied the Pecos-Jemez traditions. He learned the Towa dialect from the Tanoan language group. The words themselves, their inflection and the vocabulary, formed an important thread of his culture.

He learned that the *cacique* was an honored man, the spiritual leader in his pueblo, (functioning much as Moses did during the wilderness wanderings) and found that whenever a pueblo was established this spiritual leadership was indentified immediately. It was the *cacique,* in point of fact, who decided whether a transfer to another location might be needed by the tribe due to the deprivation of their land, decimation of game, scarity of rainfall, or terrible fires. He established the basic Indian philosophy and belief.

The child heard his mother instruct him that he was never to forget that he was a member of a certain clan. He thus had a right to participate in the political and social structure of the pueblo. He was a member of a religious group because he was a member of a certain clan, a family designation. His mother's clan designation was passed on through her family and had been since the beginning. He saw love as it permeated his life in manner, communication, and attitudes of his group.

He witnessed love and caring expressed in many ways. When, by some circumstance, the fire which had been banked carefully at night refused to be coaxed into action the next morning, the woman of the home took a small shovel or other implement and went to a neighbor to borrow fire. It was gladly shared. If they were away from the pueblo, the lad saw older men making fire with a drill or flint or using metal against metal. Although the fireplace was used for warmth and for cooking, it also furnished light for their home. Interior rooms were lighted by cottonseed oil based lamps.

He viewed the potters at work, molding the beautiful ceramics and pottery and cookware. He knew that they would later be used for preservation or storing of their food, or cooking, or even serving.

He passed the two kivas in the pueblo and gradually learned that the Jemez was a bi-social grouping, consisting of the turquoise and squash moeties. This allowed a sense of belonging to a smaller group and provided for competition in races and games as well as variety in their dances and ceremonies. His parents and grandparents were examples of these social patterns that made them viable members of their society. And looking on, he acquired by observation and communication, by attitude and nuance, his heritage.

It began as a gentle breeze, stealing across the pueblo in almost indiscernible fashion, crossing a threshold here and there. But then, gaining in momentum, it began to tear its way into their valley, increasing in devastation, decimating the populace, and wreaking havoc with their quiet, gentle manner of life. Day after day the death toll rose. Those well enough were spending their full time digging the graves for the still bodies which seemed to increase at a faster pace than the burials could be carried out. And when, at last, the relentless fury was spent, the Jemez was more hushed than it had ever been before. The remaining Indians stared in wonder at their increased burial ground and then at their fragmented tribe. The influenza epidemic which had chiseled its way across the face of the earth in 1918 had made its visit to the Jemez.

Intermittently, smallpox ravaged the group, leaving empty places in their homes. Infant mortality took its turn as mothers fought for the lives of the children on their knees.

Nevertheless, the life which remained continued in much the same fashion as it had for hundreds of years past. José Rey Toledo, only three years old, knew that there were few playmates around, but was too young to realize then that the huge generation gap caused by disease and devastation could never be erased. It would always remain. His own mother eventually gave birth to fifteen children, but reared only four to maturity. The extreme poverty in the tribe, the lack of pre- and post-natal care, lack of proper immunization and chronic illness all took their toll on the pueblo. His mother became a practicing healer, seeking to assuage a part of their pain. She was the equivalent to the Spanish *curandera* as she went about the village administering poultices, emetics, caring for tubercular patients, and serving as midwife. She went, as needed, from house to house in her wonderful care of the sick.

When José was five or six years old he was sent to the nearby San Diego Mission School, a parochial school run by the Franciscans. It was a convent school, conducted by the priests and nuns. The support was shared by the Federal and state governments although two-thirds of the curriculum was in relation to the diocese! During his years at the school José served as an altar boy, and although he was extremely interested in acquiring an education, he often feigned stupidity in order to get along with his peers. He didn't want to seem too different!

Completing the fourth grade, a playmate enticed him to consider enrolling in the Federal Boarding School in Albuquerque. Over one thousand Indian boys and girls attended the school, which provided within its iron-fenced walls the opportunity to complete high school.

"They have tasty gravy every day and they often look like soldiers," the friend tempted. "And they have lots of music they march to and they show moving pictures of Rin Tin Tin and cowboys and Indians on Saturday nights," the friend continued, dangling the school's treasures before José.

"I had never seen a movie," José recalls, "and I liked gravy!" So he decided to go.

His mother grieved to think of her young son leaving home, but his father wisely told the lad that it would open a whole new world to him. He told him that the opportunity was great and should be valued. The father's insight into the future confirmed the boy's desire and decision to go away to school.

He found many tribes represented in the Albuquerque school, which gave him a wonderful opportunity to mingle and learn of the other Indian groups. He also discovered a military-type structure of order in the institution. It was half vocational and half academic in its instruction, and sure enough, on Saturday nights, movies were shown!

The older boys drilled with guns and on dress parade marched grandly to the music of John Philip Sousa. The higher official stood around looking for all the world like General Pershing himself as the students, clad in World War I surplus uniforms, looked on.

No Indian language was to be uttered. Those caught at such unseemly behavior were summarily punished. The desire was to totally equip the Indian child to live in the European-influenced white man's world. But they could not control every facet of life, when the students were in the privacy of their own rooms they spoke their native tongue with great relief and vigor and perhaps a bit of rebellion, as well.

The younger children were given housekeeping and yard chores to perform, but at the ninth grade level they were allowed to select a vocation for which they would be trained during their remaining school years. José was guided in shoe and harness repair and worked in this leather craft for three years. Harness repair was a real priority in those days, but he never made a single shoe for himself. His interest was somewhere else. He wanted to be a pipe fitter. And he dreamed of becoming an artist.

Professionals from the University of New Mexico went to the Indian school one day each week to teach the students. Some of the pupils were extremely gifted. The Hopis were especially adept in painting while the Acomas were fine potters. The Navajos excelled as weavers and silversmiths.

Entreating the disciplinarian (later called boys' counselor), José begged to be allowed to study art. But the man saw no future in art and felt José would be much wiser to study pipe fitting. This crushed the lad who subsequently did as little as possible in the steam fitting business, although he did have the terrible job of removing the clinkers at night. That molten coal which fell on the grate was almost impossible to dig out, and in the daytime, José sneaked over to the art department to do whatever he might be allowed to do!

At last the disciplinarian gave up, seeing that José's interest had not abated in the least. And though he was never able to work with one of the university's teachers, he did learn some fundamental processes of art. His work in tempera gained recognition from two of his valued instructors. These civil service teachers, knowing it was time for him to graduate, told him that he must continue in art, it must be developed, enhanced. Their encouragement and evaluation of his talent was sufficient that he felt he must, indeed, further this ability.

Over the next several years there were numerous changes in the life of the young artist. After attending the University of New Mexico for one year, he married a girl from his pueblo that he had met at the Indian School. They returned to the Jemez in order to provide for their family responsibilities, but they were met with many difficulties which they attempted in vain to cope with.

No longer was the barter system in effect at Jemez. Money was required to secure the necessities of life. Because of the growing population in the

121

pueblo, there was less land to go around. Consequently, the earth alone could not support its people. The war began to make inroads psychologically and emotionally, while the depression among the minority groups became an oppressive reality which could not be ignored. The Toledos found themselves torn between their strong Indian heritage and the job opportunities available to them outside the pueblo itself. And during a time when many of his peers were turning to alcohol as an escape, José Rey Toledo did the same.

Seeking companionship with those enduring the similar economic buffeting, increasing numbers of his friends turned to drink. It seemed to put a "snow job" on whatever one's problems seemed to be and then later it aided him to reach a new plateau of euphoria as its baffling and cunning elements served to deceive him in its temporary and imagined psychological detours from reality.

His mother, by now a Christian who, though unable to read the Bible, nevertheless understood its veracity, began to pray for him. She knew that the strength she had found in Christ could belong to her tortured son.

The young husband and father found himself sinking more and more into despair and held less hope with each passing day of a solution to his growing problems.

"But, thanks to Almighty God," Mr. Toledo declares today, "there were evangelicals coming into the pueblo and occasionally I would see Reverend Lee Roebuck. One day he knocked on my door and asked me if I wanted to hear the good news. Thinking he meant a job opening, or some other economic benefit in the pueblo, I said, 'Sure, I'd like to hear the good news!' "

To his great surprise the visitor pulled a red pamphlet from his pocket and began to read: "For God so loved the world, that he gave his only begotten Son, that whosoever believeth in him should not perish, but have everlasting life" (John 3:16).

The missionary continued to read, and when he had finished, his host said, "I thought you had good news!"

"But don't you think that's good news? You have many problems, but God sent his Son."

The troubled artist was sorely disappointed. He had thought there was good news for his economically deprived family. He wanted immediate help. He wanted material help.

Nevertheless, it gave him food for thought. It seemed an opportunity for the rebuilding of his character, for the restructuring of his life's philosophy, for a new outlook and a fresh hope. He knew himself to be spiritually impoverished.

Missionary Roebuck continued to visit him over the next few weeks and Miss Pauline Cammack also called on him. With each encounter new food for thought, for better living through spiritual teaching, seemed to arrest his attention. He was strangely drawn to the truth they laid before him.

Within a short while a revival meeting was announced at San Ysidro, a little Spanish village near Jemez Pueblo. Unable to have services in the Jemez itself, the missionary had rented a small adobe building a few miles away and advertised the services. Although living in Bernalillo and working with the mission there, he also visited the nearby pueblos, sharing the gospel with them.

One night during the revival, José Rey Toledo walked in and sat down quietly. In rapt attention he sat as the preacher drew his text from Matthew 16:26: "For what is a man profited, if he shall gain the whole world, and lose his own soul? or what shall a man give in exchange for his soul?"

The message seemed to burn its way into the young man's heart as he considered that he "had nothing that would gain the world, but I had something that would lose my soul." When the invitation was extended, he was surprised to find himself walking down the aisle toward the preacher. He was joined by a white lumberjack who had come down from the mountains to buy groceries, and remained to find the Bread of life.

Mr. Toledo felt a wonderful new emotion of rejoicing, a spiritual uplift, and knew he had something on which to build a better life. "I had known Christ in ceremonial form," he recalls, "but not as a living embodiment of one who came to redeem and purchase a lost item in man when man disobeyed him." He had long known of Christ's physical birth and his suffering and death, but the religious leaders he had previously known only went through the ceremonial functions. He had never before realized that Christ should be a part of his existence! Amazingly, it was only a matter of weeks from his first encounter with the Baptist missionaries until his conversion experience. "It didn't take long," he remembers.

Coupled with his joy was a counter emotion: fear. He was faced with a supreme challenge, that of facing so-called friends and his various surroundings, which in no way under the sun related to his new experience. His ambivalence was further intensified when he considered how his new found faith could be put to work within himself while blending harmoniously with others who were not seeing the things he was seeing.

Returning home, he shared with his wife that which had happened to him. She felt that he had taken a serious step as well as a terribly wrong one. She was bewildered by her husband's departure from all they had known. And as he moved among his friends, he came to feel very quickly that he had lost friends, and not gained them. He was only beginning to experience that which the apostle Paul verbalized almost two thousand years before when he wrote to the church at Philippi: "What things were gain to me, those I counted loss for Christ. . . . for whom I have suffered the loss of all things" (Phil. 3:7–8).

During the next year, however, the attitude of his wife and family slowly changed as his vibrant faith penetrated their home. At the end of that period he and his entire family were baptized by Missionary Roebuck at the Spanish-Indian Mission. "I could have been an alcoholic if I had not turned to Christ," Mr. Toledo says, reflectively. "We must turn to Christ if there is going to be any change which will lead from bad to good spiritually. It worked for me. And it will work for others. But we can only persuade others and witness to them. We cannot decide for them."

A friend from New York came to the pueblo to help during the absence of the Presbyterian minister. Mr. Toledo attended the Bible studies conducted by the assistant, even though there was considerable harassment and disruption of the sessions. But the assistant watered a new thought growing in Mr. Toledo's mind. He must return to school. Leaving him one hundred dollars with which to get started, the friend returned to New York. Not wanting to become obligated, Mr. Toledo could not accept the offer and secured a combination loan-scholarship instead. He left his wife and children at Jemez and went to Albuquerque, sixty miles away.

It was an exceedingly difficult time for him, as well as for his wife and children. They barely sustained themselves and only with the help of relatives in the pueblo did they actually endure the hardships attendant on his continuing education.

But the artist felt himself improving in his craft and it was an exhilarating experience. He knew he was equipping himself to provide a better life for his family—if they could just hold out! And when he tucked his bachelor of arts degree under his arm in 1951, it was a joyful, significant occasion. He was the first from his pueblo to receive a university degree!

During those school years he taught at the Indian school in their art program and also served as dormitory attendant, for a time. He worked two or three years as switchboard operator at the school, doing whatever he could to maintain himself and his family. Upon graduation he worked full time as a classroom teacher of art for five years.

In 1956 he was invited by the federal government to become a community health officer. He was to be sent to the Sioux Reservation to work. His orientation took place on the Navajo Reservation in northwest New Mexico. The similarity between the two tribes was remarkable: they had the same economic needs, their living conditions were similar, and they were both treaty Indian tribes. Thus, in the summer of 1957, he began his work in North Dakota, and after two years was transferred to Pine Ridge, South Dakota.

His major function was to educate the people, in their dire economic plight, to a better way of life. There had been only one doctor for about every two thousand Indians up to that time, and one nurse to four thousand! Hospitals were located only on the more progressive reservations. As part of a community health team (consisting of a doctor, a nurse, a nutritionist, and a health educator), he went into the homes and explained nutrition, better sanitation methods, and what was to come in terms of improved conditions. And then, the nutritionist cooked a meal to demonstrate, and "we ate the lesson!"

In 1964, he was transferred to the Laguna Service Unit where he developed health pamphlets. He also showed health films, conducted health campaigns, and distributed educational materials concerning nutrition, diabetes, chemotherapy, etc. He served as tribal liaison from the health services.

In 1971, he was sent to the University of California School of Public Health at Berkeley to pursue a master's degree in public health planning. It was a federally funded program for which he received an adequate stipend. Because he had somehow found time during his earlier teaching days to receive a master's degree in art, he now had three university diplomas to his credit!

During these years his wonderful art served as an avocation. His paintings were shown in Tulsa, Oklahoma, at the Gilcrease Foundation, at the Santa Fe Art Museum, and at the Smithsonian Art Museum, to name a few. His main purpose in all his work concerned the authentication and documentation of the Indian traditional ceremonies in watercolor. He realized that some of the finer nuance of meaning are being lost, but through art, they are forever preserved. Occasionally commissioned to paint, he enjoyed his free lance efforts "when the mood called for it." In his home he has a treasure trove of his work, including a handsome self-portrait. He also excels in pottery making, beadwork, weaving, and in many other art forms inherent to the Indian culture. In addition, his wife spends many hours in the tedious medium of pottery making, carefully molding and decorating the vessel to a thing of beauty and value.

While the Toledos were living in South Dakota they allowed Missionary Roebuck the use of their home in the pueblo. Services were conducted there, but opposition began to be firmly felt. Children who attended the Baptist meetings were threatened with whippings and those who left the pueblo for church services elsewhere endured strong disapproval. At last Mr. Toledo complained to the officials. He reminded them that the Constitution of the United States provided for religious freedom. If they continued to carry out their threats, it would lead to political difficulties. He explained his faith, and that he was so upset in general that he had offered his home as a result. But it was as though he had "jumped from the frying pan into the fire" because terrible persecution resulted. The man of education, gentle in manner and of great dignity in bearing, the man of natural leadership abilities, the Christian man, was barred from any leadership designation in his beloved pueblo.

At last, the impasse culminated in a lawsuit. Mr. Toledo, termed "the leader of the diversity," was summoned from South Dakota to appear before the tribal council. They told him that he was going against their tribal law to allow the use of his home for religious purposes, that he was going against his allegiance to the tribe.

He replied that there was no legal document, but just a gentleman's agreement to maintain the property and not let it deteriorate. He added that the people involved needed a spiritual uplift.

As a result of the intricate suit, Mr. Toledo signed a document stating that he was not opposed to the tribe. They told him that they had nothing against him, but that he should conform to the traditional concepts—and then everything would be all right!

In a great understatement, Mr. Toledo says, in speaking of the first Catholic inroads into their pueblo: "Although the first who came were jealous of us and wanted to retain us, denomination is not the essence in establishing my right to enjoy the promises of God. If we are going to follow Christianity, the faith we have in almighty God, and the spiritual program he has designed for us to follow, is dictated. We reap these deep spiritual benefits because we find the faith to abide by the examples set by Christ and his predecessors, who paved the way for the spiritual steps to what we are seeking. Rewards are secondary. Evangelism should not consist of glittering promises of streets of gold and pearly gates, but to plant the seed of faith exemplified by the sower who went out to sow, to share what we have experienced. The author and finisher of our faith is God. There is too much religion by convenience. We need a personal encounter!"

Today, about one-fourth mile from the pueblo lands, a Baptist church building has been erected. The Cooperative Program, through the Home Mission Board, provided funds and material for the initial building. The Brotherhood of Central Baptist Association provided men and boys to erect the structure and ladies from the Woman's Missionary Union went out to serve dinner on their workdays. It was a wonderful, cooperative effort. And Missionary James Bowen, who saw the project to its completion, said: "God has given me the talent of being close to someone who can build for the glory of God!" As a result of his contacts and friendships with committed Christians, the edifice came into being at considerably less expense than might have been expected otherwise. Churches and youth groups from out of the state helped as well, and in 1968, four additional rooms were built. The Indians themselves contributed $1,000 toward that project.

When a mission is begun by Mr. Bowen, he encourages them to give 10 percent of their receipts through the Cooperative Program the very first year! This percentage is then increased as rapidly as possible. *The Baptist New Mexican* is sent into all the homes. Through these methods the people quickly begin to feel a part of the larger world of Baptists, as contributing, knowledgeable members.

The Toledos are members and a vital part of this congregation. They attend special Bible studies and support the work done for the youth. He is moderator for the Jemez Baptist Mission and bears much of the burden for the quality and quantity of witness it maintains in the pueblo. When seminary extension courses are offered at the Baptist Building in Albuquerque, the Toledos drive into the city to attend.

Attending a Christmas program at the mission is a moving experience. Lottie Moon Offering envelopes are passed to everyone present. Familiar carols are sung. A living créche is arranged before the congregation. Although clad in beaded moccasins, silver and turquoise jewelry, and swathed in Indian blankets, bearing on their faces the unmistakable mark of their rich Indian heritage, it is nevertheless, a moving picture of the nativity and a reminder of the Christ child who cut across race and creed and color. José Rey Toledo stands behind the pulpit dressed in a rich green velvet shirt over white trousers. A beaded belt circles his waist and a matching piece catches his hair at the nape of his neck. His voice, though quiet and gentle, is nevertheless imbued with authority as he traces through the Old Testament the promises of the Messiah. He reads the Christmas story and then suggests: "Christ is often left in the manger in the pueblo!" And an answering Anglo heart reaches out

127

in recognition of the sober fact that around the world the masses of humanity pause and gaze at the manger of Christ, but they never experience Easter in their hearts! And Mr. Toledo pleads with his people to enthrone Christ in their lives as they seek to exemplify his walk on earth.

Speaking at a session of the Baptist Convention of New Mexico in Carlsbad he spoke from his well-loved passage from Matthew 13:3–11 concerning the parable of the sower. The Indian nation identifies with the soil and with all of nature and this teaching of Jesus seems especially meaningful to them. He discussed the fact that the sower was faithful to sow on all kinds of ground, but that the results were in accord with the response of the soil, the sun, the thorns, and other various impediments. He added that to some is given the knowledge of the mysteries of the kingdom of God, but to others it is not. He mentioned the fact that Christ stresses the sowing of the seed (the Word of God) and adds that the germinating principle of the seed in nature as well as in the spiritual realm is implanted by God alone. Man has his part in preparing the soil and planting the seed, but the rest is in God's hands. He asked whether we were as the teachers of Israel in Christ's time, who were not sowing the seed, but who rather depended on their tradition and speculation. He asked the penetrating question, "Is your teaching with power to quicken the soul?" He said that it is not safe for man to be a critic of God's work, or of the stony places where the seed is sown.

When Mr. Toledo retired in 1976, it was from an active ministry and service to his people. He traveled in their behalf as a health ambassador for his government, but he also bore a witness to his faith in Christ. And although he, because of his Christian belief and practice, was poignantly "in the world but not of it" he worked in every way he was allowed to make life better for his people.

On one trip he was sent to Alaska. The natives were not patronizing the private hospitals, although it was possible for them to do so. They suffered as a result. He represented the Indians in the conference to which he went and spoke for them. Dressed in his own native garb, it was a particular thrill for him to be in Alaska, an area from which his ancestors had likely come thousands of years before. In relation to the lack of Indian participation in the hospitals he attempted to explain the native beliefs. At the end of the meeting he prayed, closing his intercession in the name of Jesus.

En route home by plane one of the committee, a Jew, addressed him. "I was impressed by your talk, but why did you mention Jesus?"

"Why not?" Mr. Toledo quietly responded. "After all, in a physical state,

Jesus was a member of the Jewish race. When I was in California I participated in the Seder commemorating your Passover, the hardships and sufferings of the Jews. I, too, have had a hard life. My people have migrated much as the Jews have done . . . we, too, have been an oppressed nation . . ."

"We don't believe the prophet has yet come!" the Jew insisted.

Mr. Toledo continued. "Others do. And I do. Now, you asked me a question and I was polite enough to answer it. Now you answer my question."

Looking intently at his companion, an American Indian, a first American, asked his Jewish seatmate: "How does it feel to be a chosen person of God?"

The man of Israel was rather stunned. Mr. Toledo offered one last statement: "Christ is my Savior!"

One can hardly be a member of the world community today without the stark realization that not all of earth's people are free indeed. There are still restrictions, traditions, prejudices, legal entanglements, overt and covert repressions among the nations of men. It is particularly important when couched against that framework to see a freedom of the human spirit which transcends the bounds of earth's restraints. Even as Jesus when oppressed "opened not his mouth," Perhaps there is no greater liberty today for his people.

Mr. Toledo fervently holds to the tenet that Christ has already won the victory for those whom he has redeemed. There is, thus, no need for us to fight and war for that which has already been so dearly achieved. We simply share the victory! "For whatsoever is born of God overcometh the world: and this is the victory that overcometh the world, even our faith. Who is he that overcometh the world, but he that believeth that Jesus is the Son of God?" (1 John 5:4,5).

8.
Dios está de veras entre ustedes A
Doug and Jane Pringle

Across the Havana Bay from the capital city of Cuba is the town of Regla. One may take a launch across that waterway when travel between the two cities is called for, or motor around the bay. Missionaries returning to their post in Regla could choose either way, although if children were along, they normally yielded to the excitement of the young and crossed by water.

Although Dr. and Mrs. Herbert Caudill had served in Cuba since 1929, and had enjoyed brief visits back in the States, their return to Americus, Georgia, was marked by a significant occurrence. Their second daughter, Jane, was born during their visit with Mrs. Caudill's parents. Thus Jane was welcomed not only by her joyful parents and sister Margaret, but by her grandparents as well. Her grandfather, president of Georgia Southwestern College in Americus, served to offer home and stability—a place of reference—to his missionary children.

Back in Regla, the young family picked up its work where the little girls were surrounded with the richness of a double culture. At home they spoke English and enjoyed the customs and celebrations attendant to most Americans. When they were elsewhere they spoke Spanish with assurance and participated in many of the significant customs of Cuba.

The main feast of Christmas in that island country begins on the eve of December 24 and lasts long into the night. The natives feast on roast pork, rice, and black beans with all the trimmings. January 6, the day of presents for the children, is eagerly anticipated. According to their tradition, the Three Wise Men are the children's benefactors at that time.

One year, after viewing the scene with evident wonder, young Jane wrote a letter to the Wise Men asking them to bring the gifts which Santa had forgotten! In return she received a letter. It stated succinctly: "Little girls who receive gifts from Santa shouldn't expect gifts from the Three Wise Men!"

At Easter time the images and saints of the people played a large part in the celebration in the homes of the Catholic Cubans, as well as in their churches. Good Catholics had many such images in their homes and prayed to them

130

regularly. Holy Week was emphasized strongly and in their tradition there were many things they were to omit from their lives, especially on Good Friday.

Before the coming of Castro there were numerous patriotic holidays. Perhaps the most important occurred on January 28. There were huge parades all over Cuba on that day, celebrating the birth of one of their most honored patriots and liberators, José Martí.

The Caudills enrolled their daughters in the public schools, where they were well received and treated kindly by their teachers. Jane was usually the smallest child in her class. One year, she found herself sitting at the very back of her classroom behind all the larger students. Accustomed to being treated as the other children, she asked her teacher if she might be moved a little closer to the front of the room. She explained her predicament carefully, expecting the usual understanding from her teacher. But the child received her first hint of Communist feeling toward Americans when the teacher said gruffly: "You're just like all the other Yankees . . . always asking for favors." That was only a foretaste of the trauma she endured that year from her Communist teacher. Fortunately, in the forties such a teacher was an exception to the rule in Cuba.

Back at home and church she moved with more acceptance that year. She attended Sunday School during her growing up years, as well as the Sunbeams, where the needs of China and Africa especially captured her youthful attention. When a Cuban minister conducted a revival meeting in their church, in the very natural order of events, she accepted the claims of Christ on her life and was baptized into the fellowship of that church. She accompanied those engaged in a mission Bible School on Saturdays and by the age of nine or ten began to teach the Sunday School lesson to children younger than she. This seemed to reinforce the bent toward missions which first appeared in embryo as she attended her Sunbeam Band.

When Christopher Columbus discovered Cuba in 1492 he is said to have called it "the loveliest land that human eyes have ever beheld." Also called the "Pearl of the Antilles," because of its infinite beauty, the native Indians on the island—the Arawak and the Ciboney—soon found that their lives under the Spanish rule failed to match the loveliness of their surroundings. Sadly, as slaves to their captors, they soon died out completely due to the hard labor required and the diseases they contracted.

Except for a brief period when ruled by the British, Cuba remained a colony of Spain through many revolutions until they overthrew their cruel captors in 1898. The naval battle at Santiago de Cuba and the land battles at El Caney and San Juan Hill seemed to convince Spain at last that they could no longer effectively rule Cuba. When they signed the Treaty of Paris, Spain gave up all claims to the island.

The United States established a military government and set about to improve education, public works, and health. After a constitution was adopted in 1901 (which gave the United States the right to intervene in Cuban international affairs through the Platt Amendment) a president was elected and the United States withdrew, retaining only a naval base at Guantánamo. During the ensuing years various self-serving factions threatened the infant democracy as time after time new leaders seized control. But because of their good relationship with the United States, travel and trade between the countries remained strong and of mutual benefit. Americans came and went freely with no passports required and lived without fear in Cuba.

In March, 1952, Jane, by then a high school student, boarded a public bus to her classes. Everything seemed to be perfectly normal. It was only when she arrived at her school that she learned her adopted land had suffered a coup during the night. After an almost bloodless takeover of the government, Fulgencio Batista y Zaldivar was the new President.

Leaving for the United States to enter Mercer University, the Baptist school in Macon, Georgia, Jane and her family must have experienced the same wrenching emotions countless missionaries and their children have faced through the years. She flew to Miami, Florida, and then boarded a bus for the fourteen long hours to Macon. Once there, she experienced a culture shock! Although an American through and through, and though intermittent visits to the United States had been made, she had felt almost like a visitor during her parent's furloughs. But now, alone, it seemed as though she were in a foreign land!

She dug into her studies, majoring in science. She began to be in demand at various Woman's Missionary Unions to speak on Baptist work in Cuba. She became the organist for her church and was involved in a puppet ministry. And after a missionary chapel speaker rekindled the earliest yearnings in her heart, she returned to her room to pray. "Lord," she began, "you know I don't want to serve as a missionary all by myself . . . but I will, if you want me to!"

When George Douglas Pringle was two weeks old he was enrolled in the Cradle Roll Department of the First Baptist Church in St. Petersburg, Florida. His father was an active deacon who also did the bookkeeping for his church, and his mother worked in Sunday School.

During World War II homes around the world were separated as husbands, sons, and fathers entered the conflict. The Pringle home was no exception. With her husband away, Mrs. Pringle maintained the strong church relationship which had always been an integral part of their lives.

A new pastor came to their church during this period and found that a revival meeting had been scheduled. The evangelist graciously offered to step aside, understanding that the church's interim pastor had arranged for the services, not knowing how long the church would be without a pastor. But the new minister insisted that the plans continue as made.

One evening the evangelist preached a pastoral message, taking as his text the familiar passage where the resurrected Christ asked Peter three times whether or not he loved him. At Peter's repeated insistence that he did, indeed, love him, Jesus commanded: "Feed my sheep" (John 21:15–17). During the invitation the evangelist said: "Whoever will can give his life to Christ right now!"

Young Doug, eight or nine years old, for the first time in his life had the strong and strange impulse that he should yield his life to Christ, that he ought to respond. Looking up into his mother's eyes he whispered, "Does that mean me?"

133

With her heart surely leaping within her, Mrs. Pringle assured her son that the message of salvation included him!

After the two talked with the evangelist at the close of the service, it was suggested that Doug make his public commitment the following night. The minister was fully convinced that the lad knew what he was about.

As young as he was, the feeling that he was wonderfully in God's hands remained a part of his being, although he had no idea what direction his life might take. When his father returned home on leave a few months later, the boy was baptized.

Doug Pringle's decision was the only one registered during that entire week.

Mr. Pringle was involved in the Korean conflict as well as World War II. When he returned home to Florida at last, he found that there were no jobs awaiting his release from the service! He learned that the Lockheed Corporation was employing machinists in Marietta, Georgia, and when they discovered his superb qualifications, they hired him on the spot.

Moving to Georgia in the summer of 1952, they immediately joined the First Baptist Church, where Dr. Griffin Henderson (now teaching in the Baptist Seminary in Hong Kong) was pastor. Doug was completely engrossed with the splendid program for the youth in that church. The pastor and his wife were quite interested in the youth's growth and development. This was a new avenue of Christian concern and experience for him. Mrs. Henderson sponsored trips to Ridgecrest for the young people and Doug availed himself of that privilege two or three summers during Student Week. These sessions, planned with the needs of youth in mind, served to reinforce in Doug's heart the willingness to let God control his life. He came to a fuller understanding of all that was involved in committing his life to God. During one invitation he found himself praying: "Lord, if there is one here that you want, help him to move out!" The next thing he knew, he was halfway down the aisle himself! It was more than a recommitment of his life, it was an awareness steadily growing within him that God wanted him to do something definite. He still did not know where this commitment would lead him.

As he entered his senior year in high school he submitted to extensive testing for scholarship from Lockheed. The scholarship committee took its job seriously and the qualifications ran the gamut of human achievement. Only two of the coveted prizes were awarded each year and the many applicants worked hard for the reward.

At last the results were made public, and Doug Pringle was one of the recipients! Intending to become an engineer, he must, according to the scholarship, attend a privately endowed university approved by the committee. He settled on the Carnegie Institute of Technology in Pittsburgh and spent two years studying chemical engineering. He joined a fraternity and was amazed at the "intellectual brilliance yet spiritual and moral ignorance of some of the students . . . spiritually, they had nothing!" Standing aghast at his new discovery and away from Baptist influence of any kind, he reminded himself that those young men would be the leaders of industry and engineering. And once more he felt the compelling tug in his heart . . . the world needed spiritual power and moral excellence much more urgently than it needed the techniques of science.

He transferred to Mercer University where he majored in sociology, bringing enough math hours along with him to secure a minor in that subject.

Between his junior and senior years he worked with the Home Mission Board and while involved in the Board's summer program he struggled with a decision to preach. He thought he could "handle" religious education, or even music. But preaching was something else! It made him nervous to speak before people. But he couldn't be happy with his attempts in trying to "out talk" God!

One day, walking across the campus he said, "Well, Lord, if you want me to be a preacher, it's ok with me . . . but you'll have to make a preacher out of me!"

Somehow, in that simple prayer of submission, he had struck the very essence of the making of a minister: only God can mold one for divine service.

It was inevitable that the paths of Jane Caudill and Doug Pringle should cross. Dedicated to the same high purpose, with a desire to serve as God would lead, they began to feel increasingly at ease with each other and drawn together. They enjoyed the same things. More and more their deepening friendship "seemed to be right" and they began to make plans for their wedding upon graduation.

On June 7, 1958, five days after their college baccalaureate, they were married in the same church in Macon where her parents' wedding had been conducted years before. Dr. Caudill had met his new son-in-law some months previously, when he was in the States for a Home Mission Board meeting, and Doug had visited the family in Cuba. It was a mutually joyous occasion.

They moved to New Orleans where he entered the seminary, while Jane taught school. When she earned her first check, they promptly went out and bought a dinette set. They had been using a trunk for a table and odds and ends for chairs!

They enjoyed the old country charm of the city, as they strolled through the French Quarter and visited Lake Pontchartrain. They joined a Spanish-speaking church where he led the singing. He couldn't speak Spanish, but he could sing . . . and he read! Under the excellent tutelage of his new wife, he began the study of Spanish, becoming exceptionally adept, and adding it to his knowledge of French. She worked in the Children's Pre-School Day Care Center at the seminary, a laboratory of the Religious Education Department, and felt that experience equipped her in an in-depth manner for missions work with children. She also served as organist of a church during their second year in New Orleans, and picked up relevant courses at the seminary as her time allowed.

As they neared graduation, they began to work with the Home Mission Board relative to appointment as missionaries to Cuba. This had been in the back of their minds since his visit with her to that island before their marriage. While there he had asked, "Would you be willing to be a missionary wife?" This dream, this hope stayed with them during their days of preparation. With their splendid backgrounds such appointment by the Board might, on the surface, seem automatic.

When Paul admonishes us to pray for those in authority over us in government, it is no idle, off-the-cuff remark. Throughout missionary history, beginning with the apostle himself, the rise and fall of Christian missions has been at the mercy of the governments to which the dedicated went. How often have we witnessed doors being closed to nations of the world! How many times have missionaries been relocated because of threat to life, learning a new language, settling into a new culture, working with a new mission! And too many times they have barely escaped with their lives, while the blood of others has been spilled in alien lands!

In Cuba, a loud, threatening voice began to be raised against the president. Gaining followers rapidly, the rebels began in the Sierra Maestra mountains to foment strife and indulge in brutalities against Batista's forces. Bearded men came down from the mountains and ravaged the countryside. Army and police headquarters in some areas were captured. Skirmishes and guerilla encounters became frequent. Buses were stopped on the highways and burned, as the passengers watched in terror.

As the rabble increased, President Batista seemed unable to stop the rolling tide. On January 1, 1959, Batista slipped out of the country, leaving his followers in dire straits. Many were arrested and killed, while others were given life sentences in prison. Fidel Castro took over, announcing that he and his followers were on their way to Havana. People who had held disregard for the dictator-president, looked with new hope toward the bearded man, who assured them that he was their friend, that things would be better, that he was not a Communist. And they thrilled to his long barrage of speeches and cheered him as he closed with a waving fist: "Patria o muerte, venceremos" (Fatherland or death, we shall overcome).

As he sprinkled his addresses with words from the Bible, and from Jesus himself, the unwary joined his ranks with the fervent hope that a new day was dawning for Cuba. Catholics and evangelicals alike were included in the deceived.

This threw the Baptist work in Cuba into a state of alarm. Some pastors, wanting to be true to their Cuban heritage, didn't know which way to turn.

Former residents of China and Eastern Europe, who had fled to Cuba when their own countries had been overtaken by Communists, seemed to sense the turning tide. Many began to emigrate, followed by thousands of Cubans. On June 6, one of the Baptist seminary students was arrested and in September a pastor decided to leave for the States, deciding that his continued presence in Cuba was no longer advisable. Others soon followed his example.

In April, 1960, the Caudills were joined in their troubled country by their older daughter Margaret and her family. The David Fites had been appointed as missionaries by the Home Mission Board where David was to teach in the Havana seminary. And that Christmas they were joined for the holidays by their children from New Orleans, Doug and Jane Pringle.

Just before Doug's graduation from seminary, the news media announced that Cuba had been invaded. During the Bay of Pigs episode there were mass arrests, imprisonments, searching of the seminary, as well as great bloodshed. The Home Mission Board sent word to its constituents that they should be most cautious and should return home if they felt it advisable. However, Dr. Caudill, completely immersed in the work of Cuba for over thirty years and superintendent of Baptist work there since 1946, felt that his work was not finished. He had studied the promises of God carefully through the years. He had read of men and women who had followed God faithfully through trials and all kinds of danger. The thread that held all these traumas in focus was the promise that God would be with them until they had finished what he had called them to do. Engraved on his heart was the urgent message of Christ: "I must work the works of him that sent me while it is day; the night cometh when no man can work'' (John 9:4). He told his friends, "God has called me to Cuba and he has not changed his call." And to the Board he wrote, "One is never so safe as when he is in the center of God's will."

Thus, in the summer of 1961, the Pringles were refused appointment to Cuba. No missionaries were being sent there; indeed, those who remained were urged to exercise extreme caution, and to leave at their own discretion.

Knowing of their disappointment, Mr. Gerald Palmer of the Home Mission Board asked about their interest in an alternate field of service. They wanted to be involved in Spanish missions, preferably in a rural, pastoral setting. They were soon assigned to Parkview, New Mexico, where a medical clinic was maintained by the Baptist Convention of New Mexico at that time.

It is a remote area, small in population, rural in setting, and Catholic by religion. It was a hard place to begin, but it became a wonderful learning place for them as they made treasured friends among the people. And Jane Pringle, with great wisdom says, "When a place is difficult, you learn to love it even more!" They were helped to see that life isn't always what you would like it to be, you have to begin with what you have and work from there. And as they served, their understanding of their life's work . . . and of people . . . broadened.

In June, 1964, Dr. Loyd Corder of the Home Mission Board preached in a revival at Parkview. He asked Doug if he was still interested in Spanish missions, or whether he might enjoy English work. Assured that Spanish missions was still their first love, he closed the conversation.

During the summer, the Pringles attended Home Missions Week at Glorieta Baptist Conference Center where Dr. L. D. Wood, superintendent of missions in Panama, spoke of his work. Dr. Wood told the Pringles that he wanted to discuss his work with them on a personal level during the week, but the occasion never presented itself.

However, in September, Dr. Corder returned to Parkview! He questioned them concerning a possible interest in mission work in Panama. Indicating to him their possible bent in that direction, Dr. Corder returned to Atlanta.

Christmas was a happy time in Parkview that year of 1964. The Pringles, expecting their third child, were joined by her parents for that occasion. Jane's younger brother, Herbert, Jr., lived with them at that time, because his school in Cuba had been closed by Castro. Undoubtedly, the separation was more poignant than usual when the Caudills returned to their island home, leaving their son behind, their daughter's family in the throes of an important decision concerning their field of work, and facing an unknown quantity in Castro's

Cuba.

Returning to Cuba, conditions were found to be increasingly oppressive. On every block there were spies, informers, who reported on their neighbors. And there were seven Baptist pastors in prison.

In the early hours of April 8, 1965, veteran missionary Herbert Caudill opened the door of his apartment to the insistent knocking of four armed, uniformed men. They began a systematic search of the Caudill's possessions, examining intently the address books, diaries, and papers. When they left two hours later, Dr. Caudill was their prisoner, under armed guard. At the home of the David Fites, the scene was repeated.

Two months later Doug and Jane Pringle flew from Miami to Panama where he began his work as an area missionary. He worked also as pastor and eventually taught at the seminary while he served as pastor of the church at Aguadulce. Jane taught piano to the seminarians and conducted their choir.

Although beginning their work in Panama under the shadow of her father's imprisonment, his letters no doubt helped to sustain them. Allowed one letter a month to his family, Dr. Caudill rotated the messages. They were filled with his own assurances of God's protection of his life and he said "Our ministry is in prison for this moment." Although he had no Bible, his letters were filled with its promises as he sought to undergird his children. He quoted Jeremiah 33:3; "Call unto me, and I will answer thee, and shew thee great and mighty things, which thou knowest not." He referred to the Psalms and inscribed into their hearts the healing words of Paul from Romans 8:35–39:

> Who shall separate us from the love of Christ? shall tribulation, or distress, or persecution, or famine, or nakedness, or peril, or sword? As it is written, For thy sake we are killed all the day long; we are accounted as sheep for the slaughter. Nay, in all these things we are more than conquerors through him that loved us. For I am persuaded that neither death, nor life, nor angels, nor principalities, nor powers, nor things present, nor things to come, Nor height, nor depth, nor any other creation, shall be able to separate us from the love of God, which is in Christ Jesus, our Lord.

Though their father and brother-in-law had awesome enemies, they had superior allies! And the Word of God sustained them all.

In his work at the seminary, Mr. Pringle taught the young ministers who would soon be serving churches in their country. In his lectures he dealt with the call to preach. He reinforced the distinctive quality between choosing a profession, as a committed Christian, who feels that is God's place for him, and a call to the ministry. He stressed the difference between a commitment and a divine call to a special work. It may be the will of God for one to be a lawyer or a physician or a teacher. But real calling is only to the ministry. It goes beyond one's aptitude and interest to a point where obligation is laid upon one. You don't consider the possibilities—such as being successful or making money—it doesn't matter. If God calls, he has a place for the servant and he will equip him for that task. God doesn't just play with us to see what we will be willing to do. He has promised "to finish the work" he started within his minister.

Their nine years in Panama were happy, fruitful ones. They experienced joys in their work as well as in their family circle. A daughter was born to them and Mrs. Pringle's father was released from prison (to house arrest), after nineteen months, while David Fite, forty-two months after incarceration, journeyed to freedom. Their children spoke Spanish fluently, even as their mother had done as a child in Cuba, and they ingested the rich Panamanian culture completely.

Discovering that the Panamanian mission was being transferred to the supervision of the Foreign Mission Board, they were given a choice. They could remain in their locale and transfer to the Foreign Board or they could change their locale and maintain their attachment to the Home Mission Board. Jane Pringle had been associated with the Home Mission Board almost all her life and her husband had been a part of it for thirteen years. If they could be relocated—in a Spanish work!—they felt impressed to stay with their own Board. They were graciously informed that they could go anywhere in the United States where our work is conducted. They requested a reassignment to New Mexico, if there was a vacancy. They were told that the Spanish mission in Las Vegas needed a pastor, and if they felt constrained, that matter could be looked into.

They searched the map for Las Vegas, looked in the *New Mexico Magazine,* where they found numerous articles about that area of the state, and strangely, in God's wonderful economy, welcomed three ministers to Panama for the 1974 Simultaneous Crusade. One evangelist was John Ransdell, formerly pastor of Las Vegas' First Baptist Church. Another, Bernard Dougharty, pastored a mere sixty miles from Las Vegas, and the third was Bill Ware, the present pastor of Las Vegas' First Baptist Church! The Pringles were able to ask anything that came to mind about that city. In fact, Mr. Ware took the glad tidings from the Home Mission Board that if the

Pringles were ready, their work in Las Vegas awaited!

By August, 1974, the Pringles were back in the States serving the Templo Bautista in Las Vegas, an historic part of New Mexico. Some of those with whom they work are descendants of the early Spanish colonizers. Of the approximate population of 16,000, three-fourths are of Spanish lineage. Mr. Pringle preaches fluently in Spanish and serves as his own translator. His wife relates that much of their work is in English "with Spanish splattered around!" In addition to her work as a pastor's wife and her demands to speak, she translates articles for Woman's Missionary Union's *Royal Service* for *Nuestra Tarea* (Our Task).

The pastor is active in the high school booster club where he relates to other parents and the coaches alike. He has been invited into the mountains to preach during the football training camp. They conduct a Bible study and plan for dinners at the church one Sunday each month. The people love to invite guests for such events and it gives another avenue for witness.

The Pringles pour their lives into their work. They believe in staying on the field, with few exceptions, where they can be available to give continuity and stability to their work. They involve themselves in areas where their Christian witness can penetrate, but not be oppressive or suppressive to the dominant Catholic flavor. In short, they become "all things" to their people as they identify with them every day.

9.

Dios está de veras entre ustedes B
Herman Chacón

In the remote village of Coyote, New Mexico, near Abiquiu, many residents farm small acreages as they attempt to wrest their living from the reluctant soil. Wheat and beans, alfalfa, corn, and oats are grown. Cows are raised to provide beef and dairy products. It is a simple life.

The Catholic Church plays a prominent part in the people's lives as they attend mass and attempt to uphold their faith as they understand it.

Such a family were the Chacóns, hardworking, devout, and respected in the community. Morally upright, they were strong in their Catholic belief and practice.

But one day, eight-year-old Herman, pressed into duty helping his uncle building fences, was taken to an evangelical Christian service. He had never heard or seen anything like it before. The music of the gospel hymns was indescribably beautiful to the young lad and the expression of Christian love among the people was most evident. An elderly lady put her arm around his little shoulders and he could feel her caring heart as she smiled at him and talked with him. There was a difference here! He felt the Lord was very close as the Christian people met together in worship and fellowship.

Herman's father was strongly opposed to such an intrusion into his son's religious experience. The youth was learning what he shouldn't be exposed to! Even so, Herman could not easily forget the strong relationship with God those people so evidently enjoyed.

When only twelve years old, Herman began to find himself with the wrong crowd. They stole liquor and attended dances held frequently in the mountain villages. And by the time he was fifteen, Herman Chacón was drinking heavily. He worked at little jobs in order to have money for his growing and demanding habit. His best friend, three or four years older than he, had in his possession such weapons as guns, brass knuckles, and daggers. Thus the youth was afraid of no one, because his friend was so well-equipped. When fights or other meleé's occurred in the bars and the police were called, the culprits would be scattered completely by the time the officers arrived.

Sometimes people were actually killed in such fracases, being shot or even stoned to death. And although Herman never was a part of this fearsome activity, he witnessed such repeatedly.

In order to have more money to buy alcohol, Herman, at the age of seventeen, went to work in the atomic city of Los Alamos. In 1946, he felt fortunate to earn a dollar an hour as he worked for the Zia Construction Company. Living in Española, about twenty miles down the mountain from Los Alamos, he commuted on government buses each day. He made new friends in Española and many days as he returned from work they found their way to the bars and drank until after midnight. With this heavy schedule and this habit of life, the poor youth became ill. It became progressively apparent that his job was in peril, as his condition worsened.

Mr. Chacón had taught his sons how to work and how to be responsible and it was no doubt these lessons which helped Herman to hang on to his job at all. Even though his boss knew of Herman's drinking bouts, his work had not suffered to the point where his skill was seriously affected. He drove huge lifters which moved large sacks of cement, and he did it well.

But one day he was shaking so violently that he felt he was literally at the end of his rope. He took his lunch box at noon and sat down on a huge boulder with a fellow worker. Strangely, the man spoke in Spanish, the language

Herman understood best. And as the youth poured out his problems and frustrations to the older man he found a sympathetic ear. "I'm so sick I don't know what is going to happen to me," the lad confided. "I'm getting scared; I can't quit drinking—I'm enjoying it too much."

His co-worker said, "I have something which might help you. I have a little thirteen-year-old girl. She was born with epilepsy and had come to a point between life and death because her attacks were so frequent. But I heard that a man in Las Vegas, New Mexico, by the name of Frank Castor could pray. And I heard that his prayers were answered. I took my child to him three times. He is an ordinary Christian from Old Mexico, an old coal miner, and can neither read nor write. But after he prayed for my little girl, her attacks left completely!"

Herman warmed to the beauty of the man's story. For the very first time he had hope that his awesome problem might be solved. A peace of mind which was inexplicable flowed all around his being. For a moment he felt the Holy Spirit's compulsion: "You do it, too."

Back at work that afternoon, the peaceful feeling soon dissipated. He forgot the name of the man from Las Vegas and a few days later his fellow worker was transferred to an unknown location. Herman could not remember his name, nor did he ever see him again.

Two months later, the job he had struggled to keep was lost! He was out of work because of his drinking habits! He returned home to Coyote, where he spent the winter extremely ill and unable to work at all.

In the spring of 1948, Herman went to Colorado to work with his brother. And even though he occasionally thought of the man in Las Vegas and clung to the hope that he might somehow be helped, the man's name had been completely forgotten with the passage of time and his illness.

A Spanish proverb says: "You jump from the fire into the ashes!" With his move to Colorado, Herman did just that. He was farther from Las Vegas— and hoped-for help—and closer to collapse from drinking. After work most days he and his brother drank hour after hour in the bars and then bought a gallon of wine to take home with them, where they continued to drink.

One morning after a night of such activity, Herman awoke with a terrible hangover. His head seemed to be bursting. He went for a walk in the fields in the vain hope of some relief. He knew that the devil had him in a vise-like grip and there seemed to be nothing he could do to escape his dilemma. All of a sudden a thought that seemed to be from heaven pierced his thoughts . . . "this is the man!" And he remembered the name! Frank Castór! He raced to the trailer where he lived and wrote the name down quickly, before he forgot it again. Hope was rekindled once more as he put the paper with Mr. Castor's name inside his wallet.

After a month or so, he returned home. The crops were harvested, and Herman had about decided he would go to Las Vegas, although he had never been there before. He asked his brother to go along. The two boarded a bus and when they reached Española they rented a hotel room to spend the night. The brother was puzzled by Herman's strange behavior and asked him why he wanted to go to Las Vegas. When Herman attempted to explain his reasons, his brother couldn't sleep at all because he thought Herman was going to die!

Reaching Las Vegas the next day, they began looking for the man named Frank Castór. They went to two or three different addresses, each as fruitless as the last. Mr. Castór had moved several times. But at last, the directions held and Mr. Castór himself appeared. He had been out of town and had returned only a week before. "I almost missed him," Herman remembers, "but it was in the plan of God that he be there."

"Are you Mr. Castór?" the youth asked.

"Yes," the man replied. "What can I do for you?"

Herman was wearing a very long coat which held, in the inside pocket, a pint of whiskey. However, Mr. Castór didn't berate him, but invited the brothers inside. They had been drinking all along the way.

"I worked with a man in Los Alamos," Herman began. "He told me that you prayed for his little girl and that God healed her. I want you to do something for me . . . I don't know what!"

"Yes, I remember the girl," Mr. Castór replied, as he looked at the poor youth before him, confused and ill and depressed. Herman was now at the end of the way. Mr. Castór was his last known hope on earth.

"I do pray for people," Mr. Castór said, "and if only you can believe, I can pray for you, too, but, first take the bottle out and place it in the window."

The two knelt in the humble surroundings and Mr. Castór placed his hands on the youth's head as he prayed, "Lord, by your mercy and by your grace save this man!"

And there, kneeling before God, Herman Chacón believed with all his soul. He was jubilantly happy and at peace as he returned home. It seemed that everything would now go well with him and he determined to give himself completely to becoming the very best Catholic he possibly could. He became extremely jealous for the Catholic Church, very defensive, and he entered into the trappings of every phase of the church with great determination.

However, none of this affected his brother's life. "Don't ask me to go back to Las Vegas!" he ordered.

But Herman was pulled back as though by a magnet a week or two later. Mr. Castor could see such a difference in the young man of nineteen, and began to teach him the things of God. Years before, Mr. Castor had become associated with a black preacher in the mines of Colorado and the minister had taught him great Bible truths. He also read to him and Mr. Castor had learned many portions of Scripture from memory. And he knew that God answered prayer.

When Herman became a Christian he promised God that he would never smoke or drink again. But he omitted dancing—he enjoyed that activity so much that it seemed incredible that he could survive without it. And so, when the next dance was announced in Coyote he began to reason with the Lord— but he attended the dance nevertheless. "I didn't promise I wouldn't dance," he told himself.

About eleven o'clock that evening someone came to him and marvelled that he was still sober at so late an hour. But Herman didn't tell him why. And the "friend" continued, "Let's go out to my car and have a drink." Again, the eternal deceiver entered the drama as Herman thought, "Lord, I didn't promise I wouldn't drink; I promised I wouldn't get *drunk!*" And he followed the friend out to his car for just one drink.

When this same invitation was put to him later that evening, he felt cornered as he followed this would-be friend outside. But that drink seemed to blot everything out of his mind and the next morning he awoke in a strange car in the middle of nowhere. And he was alone. He didn't know how he had come to that spot, and he didn't understand why he had not frozen to death in the frigid January temperatures.

Somehow he made it home. He was completely dejected. It looked as though God had gone out of his life for good. He had failed miserably because he had told God that he would not get drunk and his promise had been broken to smithereens. He couldn't pray, he couldn't weep. He was drained of feeling. He was nothing more than a block of wood, dead, and lifeless. He walked outside and made his way to the top of a hill and knelt down to pray. "What can I do now?" he wondered. "Why did I do it?" He couldn't say "Our Father." He didn't deserve that. The whole world, it seemed, had turned black on him. And the sky was brass. Furthermore, it was his own thoughtless doing.

Suddenly he remembered his friend, Frank Castor, and the warm memory of his prayers was used by the Holy Spirit to touch the wellspring of Herman's penitent heart. He began to weep and to pray in earnest, promising God that if he would deliver him from that terrible evil "I will not smoke *or* drink *or* dance any more. And when I said that, a load of a thousand pounds flew from my heart . . . and for twenty-eight years I have kept that promise to the Lord. I still live by that grace!"

The change in Herman's life was dramatic and his peace was wonderful as he made monthly visits to Mr. Castor's home for spiritual guidance and help. And when he went into the service of his country during the Korean War he moved the two sisters who lived with him into a house in Las Vegas, so they could be near Mr. and Mrs. Castor.

Herman strengthened his desire to become a good Catholic. It was all he knew. He was faithful to the Church and he prayed with the priest. But soon he discovered that he had more to offer the priest than the priest had to offer him! This troubled and bewildered him and as he entered military life he diligently studied the Bible and was further puzzled about some of the biblical truths as they related to his church.

After the war he returned to Las Vegas to live. He bought a little house with money he had saved while in the army and realized he must have a job. Mr. Castór said, "I'll pray for you . . . but why don't you go to Montgomery Ward this morning and see if they might need someone . . ."

Herman Chacón did just than. He discovered to his amazement that the employee who mounted tires for Montgomery Ward was ill that day and the assistant manager told Herman that he was delighted that he had come. "I'm short of help and I will give you a job until my other employee returns." That employment lasted nineteen and a half years! Subsequently Mr. Chacón became manager of the warehouse and then manager of three departments in the large store.

Several times a week the contact with Mr. Castór continued. Herman continued to pore over the Spanish Bible that Mr. Castór had sent him during his days in the service. And, being a little unsettled over the Catholic doctrine he began to attend a little Baptist mission with friends. After a while he was going to his own church about twice a month and to the Baptist church the other Sundays! He continued this practice for several years.

During this period he met John Ransdell, pastor of Las Vegas' First Baptist Church, and Leland Warren, a missionary. Their friendship and interest in him developed to the extent that Herman found himself attending the Baptist church exclusively. At last, through his long study and strong conviction, he asked for membership in the First Baptist Church, and was baptized into the fellowship of the church.

For some time Herman had prayed that God would send him a Christian wife, one who could share with him his strong desire to serve God. As he attended the First Baptist Church he met the sister of two of his fellow employees from Montgomery Ward. She wanted to be a missionary nurse. She was the answer to his prayers and in 1963 Herman and Rosabell were married.

As they taught Sunday School classes and did missionary work in Las Vegas with their pastor, Herman felt the strong compulsion of God to preach. He knew that he must have additional education if he was to serve effectively.

Herman and Rosabell made a trip to Denver while on their vacation. A new Montgomery Ward was opening there. If he could transfer his work from Las Vegas, he could attend Western Bible College, a branch of Moody Bible Institute. But when he arrived at the new store he found fifty people ahead of him waiting for interviews, relative to employment. Amazingly, the manager was the same man who had hired him in Las Vegas years before, a Mr. Watson! He sent for Herman immediately and passing the mass of people waiting for interviews, he faced his old employer once more. Mr. Watson had been sent to open the new store from Oklahoma, where he had been located since his transfer from Las Vegas. He gave Herman a job on the spot, saying, "With all the experience you've had, I'll put you in departments you already know thoroughly."

Resigning from his position in Las Vegas, the Chacóns joyfully made the move to Denver and enrolled in school. Herman was able in four hours of work a day to earn more than he had made in eight in Las Vegas.

The Chacóns were accepted immediately into every phase of school life and basked in the Christian friendship and learning opportunities. The only Spanish couple enrolled in the school, they were "spoiled" by the student body and faculty alike.

The only cloud on their horizon was Rosabell's increasing fatigue and illness. She had suffered a terrible bout of rheumatic fever as a child and the debilitating effects of that disease was causing more and more discomfort and alarm. However, their commitment was to prepare for mission work and they asked God to help them. They were in school in terms of their call to service, not in terms of health, and many days Herman almost had to carry her up the hill to their classes.

One day the president of the college called Herman into his office. He told him that he realized Rosabell had a serious health problem and assured him of their interest and prayers. "There is an excellent hospital here," he added, "and some top heart specialists." The president then offered to accompany them to consult with the physicians.

After the doctor examined Rosabell he asked them, "What are you doing here in Denver?" "We're going to school," they answered. "What school?" he demanded. And they told him that they were planning to be missionaries and were preparing themselves through their attendance at the Bible College.

The doctor shook his head gravely. "You can't be a missionary unless you let me fix you up," he told Rosabell firmly. "You need an operation very badly . . . in fact, you need to be in the hospital right now!"

Her young husband said simply, "We just came to Denver to do the Lord's will. We are almost through school, but if you know best we can go to the hospital right now."

The doctor considered the situation carefully and then answered, "With proper medication, I believe we can carry her for a month. I'll get your wife in immediately after school."

The Chacóns managed to get through the month, completing their courses on May 31. Rosabell entered the hospital the next day and other patients were delayed while her more pressing case was taken care of. She had extensive open heart surgery on June 3, and today is in almost perfect health. When she returns to her doctors for periodic checkups she is always told, "That is the most beautiful job I have ever seen." The Chacóns fervently believe that their stay in Denver had a two-fold purpose in God's splendid plan: to prepare for Christian service, and to take care of their urgent medical needs.

After Rosabell was well enough, Mr. Watson transferred Herman back to the Las Vegas store. He desperately needed to get out of debt, incurred by the heavy medical expenses. In his hours away from the store, Herman busied himself with missions work until at last he was offered the pastorate of Templo Bautista in 1968. He served that church until 1973, and experienced the wonderful leadership of God during that time.

In 1973 he was invited to accept the pastorate of Primera Iglesia in Las Cruces. In the years he has been there the church has become completely self-supporting, one of three Spanish churches in the state to attain this distinction. They have eight groups of ladies enrolled in their Woman's Missionary Union—a total of sixty-eight ladies. They have a Brotherhood chaired by a chemistry professor from New Mexico State University. Their choir recently purchased a piano for the neat, well-kept sanctuary and is currently in the process of buying choir robes. They are planning expansion of their nursery facilities. Herman Chacón is leading in a positive, vibrant ministry and is a wonderful tribute to his spiritual father, who could neither read nor write. But most of all, he is a living testimony to the power of God to transform lives from desolation into something of beauty and worth in the kingdom of God.

10.

Here Am I
John Ransdell

Young John Ransdell dressed quietly in the cold predawn morning, slipped out into the lifting darkness, found his waiting pony, mounted him, and rode into the nearby woods. Time after time he stopped, running his traps, to see whether an unwary fox, muskrat, mink, raccoon, or an opossum might have been snared since the traps were last checked. If so, he skinned the animal, stretched its hide on a curing board, and when he had a supply, exchanged them in the nearby town for cash. This money, in turn, was translated into clothing for the high school youth, affectionately called "Dub."

The firstborn of George and Laura Belle Ransdell, the log cabin which served as his first home near Milton, Kentucky, provided a close, intimate contact with nature. He gathered wild hickory nuts and walnuts in the woods. He helped his father with the numerous tasks of the farm and drank deeply of the aroma of newly mown hay.

During these years he was taken to church by his godly parents. Morally strict and upright, they read the Bible to their growing family on a regular basis. John knew that it was the Word of God, that it was divinely inspired, that it was infallible, that it contained the truth. Still, there was little need felt on his part for anything more.

Sometimes, reflecting on the wonderful things he had to enjoy in his surroundings, he knew that God was his great benefactor. God was the provider of all good things. He was the Creator of the universe. He was the sustainer. By him all things lived and moved and had their being. But deep within himself, while acknowledging the earth's bounty as a gift from God, he was not moved to place God in his own life. Even though he moved by nature, there was a lack on his part in asking for any kind of help, nor were his ears sensitive to suggestions that he listen to an explanation of the way of salvation.

Suddenly, everthing changed. It came without warning, completely unheralded and unexpected. His mother, a vital presence in his life who had tenderly rocked him and her six other children before the old fireplace and wood-burning stoves when they were small, and tenderly cared for them as they grew, was delivered of her eighth child. Within three weeks, she was dead. She was out of their lives forever. Only their vivid memory of her remained.

And so, at the age of thirty-nine, George Ransdell was a widower with eight children to rear, one a mere infant. Seventeen-year-old John, looking on the tragic, inexplicable scene through eyes misty with his own sorrow and loss, marveled at the strength and determination of his father. Deeply bent by his agony, he was nevertheless not broken, and firmly resolved to rear his children as a family. They would remain intact!

As they attempted to take up the slack and proceed without Laura Belle's gentle presence, John saw a veritable miracle unfold before his eyes. His father's stalwart character, though tried to the core of his being, remained firm and strong. Only God could enable a man to do all that George Ransdell was able to do during the following years. And John knew the source of his father's strength; it was unexplainable otherwise.

When he graduated from high school, John obtained work with the Atlantic and Pacific Tea Company (A and P). He quickly worked his way up through that huge organization. He was transferred numerous times for additional exposure and training on his climb upward. By the time he was nineteen years of age he was living in Salem, Indiana, just across the border from his LaGrange, Kentucky, home. Often on the weekends he returned home to help his father with the other children, to encourage him, to be with him. However, if he remained in Salem he attended church with his landlords, Mr. and Mrs. John Green. Dedicated Christians, she was the sister of the noted pastor of Cadle Tabernacle, Dr. E. Howard Cadle of Indianapolis. He preached over the radio every morning at 6:30 and John, along with the Greens, listened to him before he went to work. Dr. Cadle was supremely evangelistic, expressing humanity's need of Christ in a convincing manner. This somehow stirred something deep inside the young businessman's soul as he listened. Even so, there was no overt response.

By the time John was twenty-one, he was manager of the A and P store in Bowling Green, Kentucky. Numerous employees worked under his direction. He was doing well.

One Sunday afternoon, seated in a car in front of his store, some friends approached him and introduced him to a young lady. She was Marguerite Lawrence who had made her home in Bowling Green after the deaths of her parents. Petite and lovely, with sparkling eyes and a friendly manner, John

couldn't shake the memory of her from his mind after their initial encounter. Soon he contacted her and asked for her company. And although she had not been completely "overcome" by her former meeting with Mr. Ransdell, she accepted his invitation.

When he called for her, she opened the door to the tall youth standing straight as a reed, slender, with coal black hair, and dark eyes. Both were vivacious and outgoing, and their friendship developed quickly and began to deepen. Before long, they began to plan for their wedding. John had been drawn to her because of her beauty, her character, and her fine family. Strangely, it was also vital to him that she was a Christian. Somehow it mattered to him, although he knew that he was not.

Joyfully, they set up housekeeping after their marriage in 1937, and he dutifully attended church with her every Sunday. In time a beautiful baby girl came into their home. They named her Gail. Beaming on her, John thought, "I must be favoring God because he is so good to me!" In no way could he realize how lost he really was, even though he recognized that all he had was a bountiful gift from God.

Throughout John's life God had been revealing himself to him: through nature, through his godly family, through sorrow, through his Word, through the church, through the witness of friends, through success, and then through his happy marriage and his tiny daughter. And when the pressures to become a Christian seemed too great he simply put the troubling thoughts behind him, saying, "Not now! Some other time."

The day after Gail's second birthday, her father contracted a cold. It lingered and lingered. He couldn't seem to shake the nagging cough. He consulted a doctor and then another. Their verdict confirmed his most terrifying fears: he had tuberculosis! He knew the death rate for that dreaded disease. He understood his chances for recovery were exceedingly remote. And he remembered darkly that every eight minutes in the United States a tubercular patient breathed his last labored breath.

Immediately, he was put to bed. He could no longer work. He couldn't go to church with his family. He couldn't do anything! He was an invalid. And he was twenty-seven years old.

Three times a day Marguerite made her way to his bedside with a tray of food to tempt his flagging appetite. In between she took care of the other innumerable daily tasks required in the comfort of her patient. His day was briefly brightened when tiny Gail was allowed to come only to his door and lift her little hand to wave and smile at him as he struggled to lift his head from the pillow to capture the full picture she made.

His heart was moved to despair as he considered his certain end. Life was choking him off, severing him from his foundations, robbing him of his duly expected years. He thought of his impending death, of leaving his wife and child. He was haunted by their lack of income and thrown into further despondency when Marguerite had to leave him alone to seek work. However, this did not—could not—last long as he desperately needed her care throughout the day. Eventually, she began to sew at home between her nursing duties as she made draperies and slipcovers for her clientele. Her days tumbled over each other, filled with service to her patient, with housework and cooking, with Gail, and with the omnipresent sewing and pressing. But if John despaired, she did not.

Day followed interminable day and there was no improvement. He read. He listened to the radio. And, in general, he felt "like a two cent piece with the two rubbed off!" He had no strength. He had nothing to hold onto except his wife and child. Even Gail could do little more than lift his sagging spirits for fleeting moments of time. He was doomed, and though he did not verbally share his despondency with his wife, he knew that he was fighting a losing battle. And he knew, too, that when he died, he was not prepared for eternity.

One day, after lying flat on his back for about six months, John asked

Marguerite if she would bring him the Bible which had belonged to her parents. It was particularly valuable to her as it held dear memories of her childhood. He decided to read it from pure curiosity, having read almost everything else within reach.

He first read the book of Genesis and proceeded in orderly form, page after page, through the Old Testament and into the New. He read to the last word in the book of the Revelation. He had not read the Bible for years, but in the quiet stillness of his room, God spoke to him in dramatic and forceful words which leaped from their pages and lodged in his heart, piercing, cutting, and convicting his soul. His plight was infinitely worse than he had feared! God's judgment was sure; his word irrevocable. But his promises wove their golden thread of comfort throughout the Bible. There was hope! And John, in his weakened and impaired state, felt God's powerful work to the depths of his being.

While his family was out one day he came to the third chapter of the Gospel of John. He read the story of Nicodemus and Jesus in that passage which contains enough gospel truth to redeem the whole world. He read Jesus' insistent reply to Nicodemus' urgent question concerning how he could be saved. It was simple: "Ye must be born again!" (v. 7). John stopped reading and laid his Bible down beside him. He looked toward the ceiling of his room—that familiar ceiling—but through it, somehow, on into heaven. From his pillow he talked with God. "Lord, I haven't been born again. If I were to die without being born again, I'd go to hell." And right at that moment he gave his heart to Christ! He was born again! And he was unutterably happy in spite of his physical plight. He was a Christian and knew almost immediately that when God had not been able to get his attention in the many blessings of his life that "God somehow put me down in order to wake me up!" And he was able to praise him for it.

When Marguerite returned home, he shared the jubilant news with her. Death was no longer his hovering enemy, although it remained a very real threat to him. And it seemed that God literally numbed their feelings so that they could accept the possibilities that otherwise would have menaced their days. While Marguerite never felt that John would die, he came to accept the probability with grace. And found it to be sufficient!

Even in the face of the lingering illness, even when the physician's report was worse than the one before, there was never the feeling of defeat. They never discussed their dilemma negatively; they maintained a positive attitude. And they found that the grace which God gave them to face each day was adequate. The presence of their little daughter gave them a real purpose for holding up, for keeping things together. Through it all they had their home, they had Gail, they had each other, and they had their mutual trust in God.

As soon as the doctor would permit, John attended church one morning, made his public profession of faith, and was baptized by the pastor, Dr. R. T. Skinner (who later left Bowling Green's First Baptist Church to accept the editorship of Kentucky's Baptist paper, the *Western Recorder,* where he served for many illustrious years). John attended—and joined—the *Agógé* (manner of life) Sunday School class and was able to attend it only the one time. But he was elated nevertheless over God's provision for baptism and church membership. Two weeks later, however, he became desperately ill with pneumonia. Though certainly not connected with his exposure at the time of immersion, it was a serious setback to his waning strength.

At that time it seemed that Marguerite had to seek work outside the home. She worked for some time and then she became ill! Her doctor insisted that she must rest for six months! Stunned, they sought care for their little daughter among relatives and the young mother put herself to bed.

Was illness to be their constant, all-inclusive, all-encompassing lot? Permitted to be up long enough to prepare their meals, she began to mend a little faster than her doctor had predicted. But he told her that the specified rest had averted a complete break down. Illness and sorrow were no strangers to Marguerite Lawrence Ransdell, who at the age of ten had experienced the wrenching loss of her mother. And when her father died four years later, she thought to herself in her quiet moments, "God has prepared me for this."

The days stretched into weeks and the weeks became months. The months were stacked into years. They somehow maintained their sense of humor, laughing themselves out of some situations and hammering into the very fiber of their marriage strength of steel and will and caring and commitment. And the days grew until there were one thousand four hundred, and sixty. For four long years illness had stalked their lives.

In the latter part of 1943, after hearing of some people being cured of the terrible lung disorders out in the "wild and wooly" West, John and Marguerite began to cast the idea around in their own minds. More than that, they began to pray about the situation. It seemed that there was no alternative, no other course. John was growing steadily worse. Perhaps he just might live two or three months longer if they moved to the West. They certainly had nothing to hope for by remaining where they were.

They sought their doctor's advice. It upset him terribly to think his patient would even consider such a drastic move in his debilitated condition. "You just don't want to go west," he emphasized.

However, a neighbor's son who had traveled to the West some years before had been cured of his malady and became a prominent business man in Phoenix. This encouraged them somewhat. But, they had no money to go anywhere and their families did not want to overly commit themselves. In such a serious matter, John and Marguerite must make the final choice. But at last it seemed that they must at least try the only thing which seemed open to them. Leaving their friends and families and traveling so far away in John's desperate condition seemed to be the ultimate test of their faith. But God seemed to be leading them in a very definite way.

When their friends and families were informed of their decision they responded to their needs in wonderful ways. John's former competitor, of a few years back, came to him and told him that the Ransdells were to pack everything they needed to take with them. "I will pay the freight for whatever you take," he offered. Thus, they were able to keep their refrigerator (icebox), Marguerite's sewing machine, which served as their business, and a few other necessities to set up housekeeping. They sold other furnishings in an attempt to have as much ready cash as possible. The Sunday School class which he had attended only one time collected one hundred twenty-eight dollars for their tickets on the Pullman (which John, of course, had to have). By the time they boarded the train their pockets had been filled with five hundred dollars by friends and loved ones. But that was about all they had on earth.

They had to locate in a high, dry climate which was not too far south and not too far north, which would be large enough for Marguerite to build a following for her work, and a place large enough to provide a good doctor. They had prayed earnestly for guidance, running their fingers over the map of New Mexico, until they fell at last on the city of Las Vegas. They had heard that there was a good lung specialist there, and believing that God was directing them, they bought train tickets with Las Vegas as their destination. They had written the pastor of the First Baptist Church, although they did not know his name. They apprised him of their impending trip and of Mr. Ransdell's condition. They told him of their urgent need for hotel accommodations and eventually for a house, when their furniture arrived.

Gingerly, they boarded the train in February, 1944, with their five-year-old in tow. They bade their family and friends good-bye and left for the unknown. They felt as Abraham must have felt as he left Ur for a land which was to him unnamed, but would be revealed as he followed step by step. And it was the land of promise!

For two days and two nights the train threaded its way toward the West, clanging loudly along the tracks, blowing its mournful whistle at every crossing, taking its passengers to a land they had never seen before.

The train clattered into Las Vegas about seven o'clock one morning and began disgorging its weary passengers. The Baptist pastor, Russell Ware, searched the faces of those who alighted and was greatly surprised when a young couple with a small child approached him. He had expected a much older pair, but the frailty and extreme fatigue of John Ransdell convinced him of the immediate need for every physical comfort. He took them to a restaurant for a hot breakfast and then quickly conveyed them to the Castaneda Hotel for prompt accommodations. They explained their need for a hotel room for several days to the clerk. Their furniture would soon be along. But the clerk informed them that the Castaneda was not a residence hotel, that she could in no way give them a room for an extended period. Rooms were much in demand during the war years. There was a small Air Force contingent near Las Vegas and other activity connected with the bursting population in the area made their request quite impossible. There was no way she could break the rules!

Rather alarmed at this turn of events, the room clerk was told that they had just arrived by train from Kentucky. John was a patient, he had come West for his health. Immediate rest was imperative.

Her attitude changed immediately. "I came here for my health, too," she smiled. "We have just had a man check out of one of the rooms and you are going to get that room!" She added that they could stay as long as they liked.

Greatly heartened, they waited for the room to be readied, and moved in. They stayed three weeks. They found that the dining room in the Castaneda served bountiful and delicious meals. Marguerite would order one meal, take it to their room, and serve it to the three of them. It was sufficient for the whole family.

The day following their arrival, John telephoned Dr. C. H. Gellenthien. He carefully explained his circumstances and then added that he would get a taxi to take him to the hospital for examination and treatment. The hospital was over twenty miles away and Dr. Gellenthien laughed aloud at John's suggestion. "You'll do no such thing!" he ordered. "I'll come to see you!"

True to his word the doctor appeared with his pneumothorax machine and Marguerite assisted him as he administered the rather uncomfortable treatment. Air was forced into his side via a tube, requiring his ailing lung to rest. For five years the faithful doctor continued the treatment on a monthly basis. He was completely dedicated to his patient's well-being and recovery. It was a wonderful testimony to the compassion and care of a Christian doctor.

As the Ransdells were able to learn more about Dr. Gellenthien they were further amazed at God's leading them to a physician of such eminence. Dr. Gellenthien was one of the foremost chest physicians in the nation. He had authored prestigious works on the subject of lung disorders and was vice president of the American Medical Association. He cared for patients from huge corporations who sent their ailing employees to him for treatment. They further discovered that the doctor had dedicated himself to medical missions years before in a distant state. But when he became the victim of tuberculosis he saw that his dream was impossible. He made the long trip to the Valmora Medical Center where he sought the help of its founder. He became completely cured of his malady and began to work on the staff of that hospital. Subsequently, he married the daughter of the institution's founder. He knew something of the trauma the Ransdell's had lived with and wanted to alleviate the situation to the best of his ability.

About three weeks after arriving in Las Vegas the Ransdells moved into a house which was to be their home for nearly five years. Marguerite set up housekeeping once more and put her trusty sewing machine to work. When her iron tuckered out it didn't occur to her to splurge on a new one. They cost two or three dollars in those days and she needed it constantly for pressing her fabric as she sewed. She took her problem to her husband and, sitting up in bed, he transferred some of the vital parts from their less needed toaster to the iron. The result was not the greatest invention to emerge from an assembly line, but the contraption worked! And they laughed together as she coaxed her makeshift iron into action, calling it a "T Model Ford with a Cadillac motor!"

One of the first places Marguerite went after their arrival in Las Vegas was to the First Baptist Church. Taking Gail by the hand, the two made their way on an icy February morning. They were hundreds of miles from home and those dear to them, but when they reached their destination they found great warmth and love and acceptance. Although the furnace was not working that frigid morning and they huddled together in a basement room for the worship service, the people "just put their arms of love around us." It was a thrill indeed, a benediction, an added gift from God.

A few days before they moved from their hotel into their new home John began to have some very strange feelings, some unusual stirrings in his heart.

He couldn't get away from them. They would not be thwarted, nor did they diminish. He was completely mystified and dumbfounded. He couldn't ferret out his emotions—they were too complex, too inexplicable. He labored mightily with the unsettling impressions. It was hard for him to comprehend all that he was beginning to believe in the depths of his soul.

Perhaps Elizabeth Barret Browning partially described his plight when she alluded to God's mighty dealings with Moses when Jehovah mobilized him for duty:

> Earth's crammed with heaven,
> And ev'ry common bush afire with God;
> But only he who sees takes off his shoes!

In the quiet of his room, John Ransdell was having an amazing reality made abundantly clear to him. The focus was becoming sharper, the picture more distinguishable.

GOD WAS CALLING HIM TO PREACH!

But that was impossible! Utterly unthinkable! The life he had remaining must be confined to his bed. What could he do! For over four years he had been able to do nothing. Absolutely nothing! Even so, as the feelings engraved themselves on his heart, and he became more amazed at the impasse he seemed to face, he never one time bargained with God. He never said "I will preach if You make me well!" That was not a part of his obstacle nor of his restriction.

Helplessly, he cast these feelings about in his mind, trying them on for size. Nothing fit. He didn't even know what constituted a "call" to preach. "How could God mean this?" he asked himself, in utter amazement. "Why is he calling me into the ministry? He knows I'll never get out of this bed except for my trip to the cemetery."

At last, completely bewildered by his strange encounters, he shared them with his wife. He told her that God simply would give him no rest, that he had almost worn his Bible out searching, seeking the mind of God in relation to his life. "Has God brought me out West to 'work me over'?" he wondered.

Moved by his sincerity, Marguerite told him that she believed he would do what God wanted him to whether he understood it at the moment or not. His complete physical inadequacies deterred her not at all in considering God's plan for his life. They simply didn't enter into her consideration at all.

For the next two years he struggled with these haunting demands on his seemingly ebbing life. The fact that he was still alive may have proved that his move to the West was having an unnoticeable but favorable effect on his health. He wrote to numerous pastors and asked them how God had called them into the ministry. They answered, explaining that transcendent experience as well as they could. But to attempt to explain a divine call through the weak vehicle of words is but to diminish it. Most of the men simply told him to yield himself to God—and God would lead him step by step.

Several unusual occurrences began to take place which added to this mystery. He began to receive letters addressed to "Rev." John Ransdell! He began to have recurring dreams where he saw himself in a position of leading people to Christ. And he was absorbed in listening to any preacher who could be heard on the radio. His dilemma was a compulsive, compelling thing. It was a magnetic force in his life, lifting him out of himself. And it was infinitely stronger than he was.

One night about nine o'clock while his family was away for a missionary meeting, John was agonizing over his decision. He began to read from the book of Isaiah and came to the burning words of the sixth chapter: "Whom shall I send and who will go for us? Then said I, Here am I; send me" (v. 8).

Twenty-seven hundred years before, in a land thousands of miles away, a king had died. Completely devastated by this international crisis, the young Isaiah no doubt considered the awesome ramifications to his country. He knew well King Uzziah's long fifty-two-year reign and realized the threat to Jerusalem and to all Judah in the possible loss of their independence. He undoubtedly thought of the successor, weak and ineffectual Ahaz, who seemed to give away all that he tried to save. The Assyrian army had been making repeated invasions of Palestine in preparation for their conquest of Egypt. And even though Uzziah had been in his last years a leper and lived in a house apart, he had exercised strong and vigorous rule over his country, wielding a protective influence over all. And now he was dead!

In the midst of this calamity, Isaiah had an overwhelming vision of God. Jehovah, enthroned in his heavenly temple was ministered to by the ethereal seraphims who formed an antiphonal choir, singing of the holiness of God. The very foundations of the earth shook and an opaque smoke arose, preventing Isaiah from clearly beholding God. Nevertheless, he heard a great voice and the acknowledgment of the holiness of God, the contemplation of that ineffable and powerful majesty, made possible—as it always has—the subsequent worship and reverence of God! It seemed that his heart would burst as the veritable glory of God himself filled the temple.

And then Isaiah saw himself! He was undone. He was unclean. He was unusable. And everyone about him was in that same perilous state. He was completely, devastatingly unworthy.

A vision of God always renders one with a feeling of extreme inadequacy. Ironically, it is only then that God can really use us.

The voice of God brought him out of his reverie. "Whom shall I send, and who will go for us?" Emboldened by it all, Isaiah responded, as though shouting his readiness for service for all the world to hear: "Here am I! Send me!"

The experience was not mystical: it was entirely practical. The prophet had a commission from God himself. And he was given a message . . . and they must always occur in that order! Thus, armed with a call and a word, he was naturally given a job to perform. He was the mediator of the word of God until the end of his days.

John Ransdell believed himself to be every bit as useless as the young Isaiah had felt himself to be. But he was also bedfast, weak. He seemed to have nothing that God in his rich majesty could want, much less use. And yet from the farthest reaches of his soul he cried with Isaiah, "Here am I! Send me!"

At that moment there was a knock at his door. His pastor of only a few months, John Cole, let himself in. And immediately the wan patient began to disclose the amazing experience—and commitment—he had just undergone.

And to John Ransdell's complete astonishment the pastor said, "I'm not a bit surprised." No doubt the pastor himself had great faith in God to encourage a man in his parishoner's physical state. But John was willing—and eager—to do anything he possibly could for the cause of Christ.

He began to write letters to men in the armed forces. As people in Las Vegas heard about this ministry they sent names to him and he added them to his growing list. All through the war he wrote to servicemen around the world. He sent clippings from the newspapers which might interest them. He cut jokes out of periodicals and mailed them along. He included church bulletins and in every letter, carefully written in longhand, he talked to them of the things of God and their relationship to him. Many men responded as he engaged in this laborious task all the days of the war. He corresponded with a hundred men, keeping before them the matters of eternal consequence. The church, as well as some of the soldiers, helped him with the expense of mailing such a voluminous outpouring of concern and love. One young soldier sent a money order each month for a five year period. It was always for the same amount—one dollar.

Later he was elected Extension Department Director for his association. He wrote letters to the churches and urged each congregation to include an extension department in their organization. He wrote to the directors, encouraging them to be faithful. And he compiled reports for his association for two years.

He was serving!

One day as Marguerite returned home she found John's room empty! Quite alarmed, she began to look for him. It was unusual for him to be anywhere but in his bed. But soon a car drove up before their house and stopped. She recognized the familiar car of Dr. Gellenthien and the frail form of her husband as he carefully emerged from the car! The doctor explained to the nervous wife that he simply felt it was about time that John Ransdell had a nice ride—and the doctor wanted the privilege of providing it. "That was a real highlight for me," Marguerite recalls. It was a significant step forward.

Miraculously, John found himself to be increasing in strength! Soon he was able to be up for short periods, and then longer ones. At last he even attended church and then was able to join his family in services at least once a week. It was amazing! How could any family be more joyous!

About that time his pastor wrote an article concerning John Ransdell which appeared in the August 1, 1946, *Baptist New Mexican*. He told of the Ransdells' trip from Kentucky, of John's long search for health, of his becoming a Christian. He mentioned the pastors who had visited him to cheer him, but instead found one who was "running over with courage and inspiration." He added that John was able to attend church services occasionally, but was a long way from being well. "But he is *on the way!*" He outlined the ministry of letter writing during the war and the power of his prayers on behalf of their church. He told of John's wonderful stewardship of his time, even though ill, as he had studied and prepared himself. "Last Sunday evening," the article continued, "at the close of the service he walked down the aisle and took the pastor by the hand and surrendered his life to do the will of God . . . . We believe that God has brought him to New Mexico to help us in our great task of winning our state to Christ!"

By October of that year the pastor felt that John was becoming strong enough that he might preach his first sermon. He gave him plenty of time. It was to be a Christmas message. And he prepared carefully.

Before he began his message, John told the sympathetic congregation: "When Brother Cole asked me to bring a message on this date I just knew that I would be scared to death when I got up to preach. But I feel much differently. I am twice as scared as I thought I'd be!'' Again, his rich sense of humor sustained him.

Marguerite's report of that evening is more revealing: "He did well from the beginning. I knew that God wanted him in the ministry.''

As his health continued to improve he began to accept invitations to preach in the northeastern part of the state. And by the fall of 1947, the Las Vegas Church ordained him to the gospel ministry. For the next year he was able to preach in different churches almost every Sunday as his strength continued to allow. One church in particular sought him out when their pastor was away— the First Baptist Church of Springer. John was called to fill their pulpit on eleven different Sundays. And when their pastor accepted another post, John Ransdell was called to be their new pastor! He had to tease them, however, saying that he had preached twenty-two trial sermons before he moved there as their under-shepherd!

They found the people cordial, warm, and patient. And though they may have arrived feeling a little apprehensive about how everything would fit together, their fears were quickly put to rest in the gracious responsiveness of the people. No one could have been happier than they as they set about to minister to their first congregation. An added blessing during their Springer days was the birth of a second daughter, Jacque. With eleven-year-old Gail, John's improved health, and a wonderful place of service, how could life be more complete!

Seeing the many Spanish people in their area without a viable Christian witness, John and Marguerite began to seek for a means to aid them. And Dr. Albert McClellan in his book *The West Is Big,* uses their work as an example. "His plan (Mr. Ransdell's) is simple enough. He and his church made friends with and won to Christ a young Spanish mother. He did so without the aid of special language study, just by kindness and sympathy. The young woman joined the First Baptist Church and then, backed by her pastor and church, led the way into more homes and soon others had also been won to Christ and accepted into the full fellowship of the church. This is it. This is the answer. This is the remedy for our slow, long, uphill fight in carrying the gospel to the Spanish people.''

Gerald Palmer wrote about the same missionary zeal in his book *Winds of Change.* He outlines the story of a mission being organized in Springer as a result of the Ransdells' ministry and the subsequent baptism of eighteen adults from Catholic backgrounds. The influence of their work was felt in all quarters.

The longer John preached and pastored, the more convinced he became that God had brought him to New Mexico for that purpose. Life unfolded before them in a beautiful manner after their having been almost in a vacuum for six years. But it had been a time of divine preparation. They could begin to see the reason for their myriad experiences as they began to face the realities of the ministry.

In all the various ways a pastor cares for his people, John Ransdell ministered to his. Weddings, funerals, revivals, and the normal routine of church life were cared for. However, it is interesting to note that in the five years of his pastorate in Springer there was not a single death from the church membership itself! Nor was there for a year after his departure.

When their former church home in Las Vegas became pastorless the members discussed the possibility of calling John Ransdell. A cowboy, Dee Bibb, was a member of the church at that time. He had known the Ransdells during their stay in Las Vegas. He had grown up with Will Rogers and seemed to be cut out of the same cloth. "Why go through all that rigamarole?" he questioned. "Just call him up and tell him to come on down!"

Even though the church went about the procedure in the proper manner, Mr. Bibb's enthusiastic welcome was matched by the whole congregation as the Ransdells returned to Las Vegas. It was an agonizing decision for them, arrived at after much prayer and soul-searching. Their years in Springer had been triumphant ones, years of joy and growth.

One of the emphases during their nine years in Las Vegas concerned work with the college students attending Highlands University. Each Sunday after evening worship their home overflowed as twenty or thirty young people poured into their living room. They enjoyed discussion, food, and recreation. It was a bonus to their ministry as it riveted together strong friendships.

The church at Las Vegas held poignant memories for the pastor and his family. Not only was the church the oldest congregation in continuous existence in the entire state, but years before the first railroad had etched its way through Las Vegas and its environs. Here they had come when life seemed to be ebbing away and when the future portended little joy. Here he had felt his call to preach and had been ordained. Here he had preached his first sermon and enjoyed his first ministry from his bedroom. Here he had been tenderly and solicitously ministered to by his faithful physician. They tried to return something of their feelings as they lived among the people. But they themselves were blessed even more.

Unexpectedly in 1962, a call came from Albuquerque's First Avenue Church. Again they prayerfully sought the will of God. Their nine years in Las Vegas (for a total of fourteen) were precious to them, not easily given up. But they felt convinced that it was the right move to make.

For fourteen additional years, John Ransdell preached to a beloved congregation. The Fruit Avenue Church, made up of a wonderfully mission-minded people, was an inspiration to them. And through all the years, he stood ready to do God's bidding just as he had been when he first exclaimed: "Here am I! Send me!"

Not only was he active in his pastorates but he served as moderator of his association, as well as clerk. He was a member of the State Mission Board, where he was elected president. He was also named president of the Baptist Convention of New Mexico and was a member of the Hospital Board of the Southern Baptist Convention. For a time he enjoyed participating as a book reviewer for Broadman Press and was a contributor to the *Encyclopedia of Southern Baptists*. In addition to revival services in our country he preached in Canada and Panama as well. His family has served to crown his efforts as Marguerite, has been a constant source of help and inspiration, while his daughters are teachers of music in public schools.

Today when you look at John and Marguerite Ransdell, experience something of their kindness and vivacious spirit, see the tall erect frame and coal black hair of the preacher, it seems incredible that he was ever ill one day in his entire life. Just as unbelievable is the fact that he is now retired from the active ministry! But in August of 1976, he entered the ranks of those who are no longer giving full time to pastoring a congregation.

But as he is called upon for some interim service, his answer will undoubtedly be, "Here am I . . ."